Option Wizards®

Real life success stories from the financial markets

By
John A. Sarkett

Compilation of features originally published in
SFO, Futures and
Technical Analysis of Stocks and Commodities

First edition, copyright © 2012 John A. Sarkett.

Features originally published in trade publications for which permissions to reprint here have been secured, including *Technical Analysis of Stocks & Commodities, SFO and Futures.*

Futures Magazine, p 72, Top Ten Options Mistakes, originally appeared in August, 1998 publication.

Sarkett, John, "Calendar King," Technical Analysis of Stocks & Commodities ™, Vol. 30, No. 10 (October 2012), © Technical Analysis, Inc. Used with permission.

Sarkett, John, "The Queen of Iron Condors," *Technical Analysis of Stocks & Commodities* ™, Vol. 30, No. 7 (July 2012), © Technical Analysis, Inc. Used with permission.

Sarkett, John, "Backtesting Options Strategies," *Technical Analysis of Stocks & Commodities* ™, Vol. 29, No. 7 (July 2011), © Technical Analysis, Inc. Used with permission.

Sarkett, John, "Triple Theta Half the Time," *Technical Analysis of Stocks & Commodities* ™, Vol. 28, No. 5 (May 2010), © Technical Analysis, Inc. Used with permission.

Sarkett, John, "Sizing Up for Success," *Technical Analysis of Stocks & Commodities* ™, Vol. 27, No. 12 (December 2009), © Technical Analysis, Inc. Used with permission.

Sarkett, John, "Adjusting options trades with Bill Ladd," *Technical Analysis of Stocks & Commodities* ™, Vol. 27, No. 13 (Bonus 2009), © Technical Analysis, Inc. Used with permission.

Sarkett, John, "Calendar spreads with Dan Sheridan," *Technical Analysis of Stocks & Commodities* ™, Vol. 25, No. 5 (May 2007), © Technical Analysis, Inc. Used with permission.

Sarkett, John, "Double Calendars and Condors," *Technical Analysis of Stocks & Commodities* ™, Vol. 25, No. 6 (June 2007), © Technical Analysis, Inc. Used with permission.

Sarkett, John, "Double diagonals and butterfly spreads," *Technical Analysis of Stocks & Commodities* ™, Vol. 25, No. 7 (July 2007), © Technical Analysis, Inc. Used with permission.

Sarkett, John, "Time and Options Probabilities," *Technical Analysis of Stocks & Commodities* ™, Vol. 15, No. 12 (December 1997), © Technical Analysis, Inc. Used with permission.

Sarkett, John, "Trading and Moneyball," *Technical Analysis of Stocks & Commodities* ™, Vol. 22, No. 11 (November 2004), © Technical Analysis, Inc. Used with permission.

Sarkett, John, "How great traders go bad," *Technical Analysis of Stocks & Commodities* ™, Vol. 17, No. 7 (July 1999), © Technical Analysis, Inc. Used with permission.

Sarkett, John, "Force Index," *Technical Analysis of Stocks & Commodities* ™, Vol. 13, No. 4 (April 1995), © Technical Analysis, Inc. Used with permission.

ISBN-13: 978-1470109721
ISBN-10: 1470109727 (Black and white version)

Published by Sarkett Press, Division of Sarkett & Associates, Inc.
Winnetka, Illinois 60093. Cover design by author. Printed in the United States of America

INTRODUCTION

"Nine out of 10 stock, futures and options traders lose their money."

Anyone who comes in contact with the capitals markets has heard that statement. For many, it is enough to dissuade. They don't venture any further.

A few press ahead.

A few turn the old saw on its head thusly: 'one out of ten succeeds' ---- and then immerse themselves in the business of finding out why.

The burning question, and quite literally, the million dollar question: Why does that *one* succeed?

That's what we have researched and written about for years, and try to show in this little book – the "ones," if you will, the real stories of real people who took on the adverse odds and came out of the financial markets jungle with diamonds in hand. We focus on options, and we call these winners Option Wizards®, after the name of the software we developed (and trademarked) years ago to help those brave enough to tackle the options markets.

How – exactly -- did they do it? How did they win?

They, themselves, immersed themselves in training to learn the art and science of risk management, of options strategies, the Greeks, markets, technical analysis.

Then they started – small. First, paper trading, then live and breathing money, but small. They took their losses, learned their craft, and pressed on. Until they attained mastery, but with humility. Each one profiled here regards the job of options trading as one of continual learning. The same way doctors, pilots, professors and Indian chiefs and other highly trained individuals do. They never stop learning. Learn or die, some might say.

So ------ we'll stop talking here, so you can start the process or more likely add to your own process of learning.

We wish you well, and hope that you, too, attain the confident and highly skilled status of Option Wizard®.

Sincerely,

John A. Sarkett
Winnetka, IL 60093
Wednesday, February 15, 2012; updated Monday, September 17, 2012

QUOTES

When you sell a man a book
you don't sell him just twelve ounces of paper and ink and glue--
you sell him a whole new life.
Christopher Darlington Morley (1890-1957)
from his **Parnassus on Wheels**, *1917*

Life consists not in holding good cards
but in playing those you hold well.
Josh Billings, 1818-1885, American Humorist

We must be willing to get rid of the life we've planned, so as to have the life
that is waiting for us.   The old skin has to be shed before the new one can
come.
Joseph Campbell

When I get a little money, I buy books; and if any is left, I buy food and
clothes.
Desiderius Erasmus

Plans are nothing; planning is everything.
Dwight D. Eisenhower, 34th President of the U.S.

TABLE OF CONTENTS

all features by John A. Sarkett

Here's The Plan From Dan (Part 1)

Calendar Spreads With Dan Sheridan

In the first part of a series based on a seminar on option strategies with Dan Sheridan, we take a look at calendar spreads.

Options and seminars go together like yin and yang, baseball and hot dogs, Abbott and Costello. Can't separate 'em, wouldn't want to. Ten or more years ago, some of the prominent seminars focused on straightforward strategies like put selling or vertical spreads. In a surging NASDAQ market, these one-day affairs served their purpose in helping retail stock traders become more knowledgeable and comfortable with options.

Then after the 2000–01 stock market crash and with the equity markets in the doldrums came delta-neutral strategies, making money in options when stocks weren't moving — timely and helpful. You might have seen infomercials for these "wealth creation" seminars.

But not all the attendees were successful, nor even the gurus themselves. One notable "expert" expanded from giving seminars to managing an option trading fund. The fund lost 40% in six months before closing. There are and have been many, many other seminars and countless newsletters, and we've all been invited by direct mail to attend or subscribe. Or both. Some of us have, or at least been tempted.

WHAT'S TO RISK?
Now streaking across the option-trading-and-seminar sky comes trader Dan Sheridan and his Options Mentoring series sponsored by OptionVue. He focuses on the missing dimension of most options

by John A. Sarkett

seminars: risk management. That alone makes him different. Something else does, too: Dan Sheridan doesn't propose doing the education job in one or two days, like many of his predecessors; his is an ongoing program, with access to him anytime.

We've been taught that inventor Thomas Edison tried some 8,000 substances before chancing on tungsten and finally being able to devise the revolutionary light bulb. There haven't been that many options seminars, but there have been quite a few. For those who stuck around long enough (and there are those who have attended just about every option seminar given in the last 10 years), Sheridan just might be the tungsten everyone has been looking for.

But he might not seem like it, at least not at first. A natural comedian, "Trader Dan" affects a regular Chicago guy demeanor, because, as he would say, "I *am* one." Sheridan survived and thrived for 22 years in the rough-and-tumble CBOE pits. His superb risk management skills protected him and allowed him to grind out profits in markets both up and down, and those are the skills he wants to share. He's generous with his time and he tells the truth, flattering or not. What more could you ask?

Not just a market maker, though he's got lots of war stories from the pits to share and some good trading tips, Sheridan successfully traded thousands of income strategy trades for his own account over the past two decades (some 3,000 calendar spreads alone, he estimates). He also mentored a number of traders who went on to major success, some to head large trading firms.

GENERATING INCOME
Dan Sheridan brought his expertise to a recent Futures Industry Association (FIA) meeting, where he spoke on how to generate monthly income in the options markets. Sheridan began the FIA session by goring a few sacred cows: "Make the odds work for

you, not against you. Income generation is a superior strategy for 99% of traders."

When trades are managed, not just put on and forgotten, Sheridan says a trader can generate as much as 100% annualized. Some may scoff, he says, but he sees his best students doing it, grinding out 5% to 15% per month. (Not everyone does this, he says. Others make up to 7%, and those who can't follow instructions lose.) Sheridan believes if he can keep a new trader in the game for six months, earning a small percentage each month, learning the craft, adjusting the trades, and keeping the enthusiasm high, he or she will make it as a successful trader in the long term.

Options and seminars go together like yin and yang, baseball and hot dogs, Abbott and Costello.

That's the goal. To achieve it, Sheridan recommends a portfolio of six or seven income strategies each month that don't require a stock to move to be successful. He also believes in staying small, keeping the account at $5,000 to $6,000 in capital for six months, whether or not the trader can afford more.

He told the story of one trader who went large on a calendar spread, lost big, got negative on calendar spreads in particular and options in general, and then quit.

"Why did you do it?" Sheridan asked about his decision to trade big.

"Because I could," the trader, a Houston oilman, replied.

Sheridan believes if the individual had kept the faith, grinding out the profits month by month instead of going for the big score, he would most likely have been profitable and still be in the game. "This is a craft," Sheridan says. "We do it over and over."

He says he now does everything in his power to slow down his prospective traders, urging them to begin with paper-trading, then graduating to small trades. "Why do you think you can trade a $100,000 account if you can't trade a $5,000 account? Learning a craft takes time. We don't say to our college sophomore, 'Are you making money yet?' We shouldn't say that to new option traders who are learning their craft, either."

Perhaps the best thing about Sheridan's approach: It does not require a full-time commitment. Most of his traders work full-time, and he dissuades others with the available time from becoming screen jockeys. Once up and running, he estimates his students spend only seven to eight hours per month at options. "This is not daytrading," he says. "Our best students have full-time jobs." These success stories have limit orders in the markets that automatically actualize at key points. Sheridan advises traders to become expert on the contingent order capability of their brokerage platform.

TRADING VEHICLES

Dan Sheridan favors these income strategies. All are spreads — no naked options:

- Calendars
- Double calendars
- Condors
- Double diagonals
- Butterflies

If you can follow directions and apply good management, you can make a business, Sheridan believes. "If I had a group of sixth-graders, and I taught them for two to three months, and they did what I'm telling them, they'd be successful. But too many retail customers know too much. They bring in Fibonacci, and Andrews pitchfork, and this and that, and pretty soon they are overthinking, and losing."

It takes one other thing, too, Sheridan says — commitment. "Some people say, 'I'm going to try a calendar spread and see what happens.' This makes me crazy. Am I going to 'try' to open a beef stand in Chicago? No, it's a business. It's a commitment. You don't give up on calendar spreads because one doesn't work. This does not provide the diversification or the time it takes to be successful."

INCOME STRATEGIES

In the FIA meeting and during a follow-up web seminar, Sheridan provided the meat and potatoes of his income strategies. First, the definitions: "An income strategy is one where we don't need the stock to move to make money." These strategies are also known as *nondirectional*, also known as *delta neutral*.

Best candidates for condors, double diagonals, and other neutral strategies, are channeling stocks, steady, sideways movers, Sheridan says.

Like a pilot looking over his aircraft before takeoff, here's how he looks for stock candidates:

1 *Volatilities.* Less than 30 is the desired range.

2 *Industry.* Predictability. Kellogg's stock would be better than an unpredictable biotech startup.

3 *Price chart.* If there was a 10% move last week or month, ask why.

4 *When to be there.* If there are upcoming earnings dates or other special events, stay out of the market.

CALENDAR SPREADS

A calendar spread is a strategy where the nearby option is sold and a farther expiration bought — for example, sell May, buy August. Calendars give the trader an edge in decay, probabilities, risk/reward ratios, and yields:

Guerrilla Calendars

What are they? Sell one month and buy next month out.
Example:
Citigroup: $50 buy 10 November 50 calls and sell 10 October 50 calls

Is this an income spread? Yes, we hope to make money by the near-month time premium decaying faster than the second month and the stock staying in the vicinity of the short strike.

How to find guerrilla calendars: Implied volatility is between 14 and 28. You're looking to pay as little as you can for the spread.

Most desirable time to put on: 25–35 days from expiration.

Are commissions important? You bet — $1 and under should be the norm and not the exception.

Is execution important? Absolutely crucial! Don't cave in more than 0.05 off mid-prices, and be very patient at mid-prices before caving in.

Is volatility an important consideration in guerrilla calendars?
Yes, but not as important as in campaign calendars (calendars with more than one month between the near and far months). We can compromise and take implied volatilities in the middle of the one-and-a-half-year implied volatility range.

How much should we pay? When we think of guerrillas we think of paying $0.10–$0.50, which is great. There's nothing wrong, however, about paying up around $0.90. Remember the term *guerrilla calendar* refers to a one-month calendar where our idea is to take a small dollar profit and run for the hills.

Time premium: You want a time premium of short option more than 50% of long option.

Minimum I should receive for my short option: You want at least $0.30, which will usually be all time premium. Just remember the time premium of short should be at least 50% of time premium of long. That means if you sell an option for $0.30, you won't pay more than $0.60!

Picky execution: Never cave in more than $0.05 off mid-prices. Execution is crucial with these spreads.

When to take off for profit: When you've made 40% versus what you paid. If you pay $0.50, you can take off for $0.70, typically in two to four weeks.

Volatility: Implied volatility (IV) in the low to middle volatility range lasts one to one and a half years. If IV is at the high end of the range, do the stress test in the analysis page of OptionVue.

Industry: No oils, biotechs, or other volatile industries

Price: When trying to detect too much speed in underlying vehicle:

- Last week, was there more than a 5% move in one direction?
- Last month, was there more than a 10% move in one direction?
- In the last three months, was there more than a 15% move in one direction?
- In the last nine months, was there more than a 25%–30% in one direction?

If you answered "yes" to any of these four questions, consider waiting.

Earnings:

- No income spread in an earnings month. The exception would be stocks with implied volatility under 25 in the last three earnings.
- No gap over 3%

Skews: There should be no positive skew over four to five points before you put on a position. If a four- to five-point skew develops after you put on a position, take it off.

News: Check the company website and some news services. Here are the words you don't want for income strategies: "merger," "takeover," "split in the stock."

Risk management: If you pay less than $0.40 for the guerrilla calendar, leave it alone till expiration day unless you take off for 40% profit or more any time before that. On expiration day, take off the complete spread on both sides. Be careful if short option is in-the-money and time premium hits $0.05; you may get exercised on the short call. If you pay greater than $0.40 for the guerrilla calendar, take off when time premium of short options hits $0.05 unless you take off for 40% profit or more any time before that. —*J.S.*

Checklist for finding and filtering candidates

1 Use a software program that has spread-searching capabilities.

2 Short side would have 25 to 30 days to expiration to achieve maximum decay speed. (You want the option you sell to lose value as fast as possible.)

3 Keep implied volatility (IV) on both sides: buy and sell sides is less than 30. That means the stock will probably move less than 30% in one year. Typically, large stocks like IBM, UPS, GE, AIG, and JNJ fit the bill here.

4 Keep the short side out of earnings months, typically January, April, July, and October, but know your stock. Some report earnings in off months.

5 Avoid major news in a selling month — for example, an FDA event or mergers.

6 Aim for a long option near the low of its implied volatility range. This gives it room to rise, positive for the spread.

7 Sell in a near month, buy two to three months out for opportunity to roll. (Rolling is buying in the near month, and selling a month farther out, or buying in a nearer strike and selling a farther strike.) The farther out the long option, the lower its volatility should be. If the volatility on the far option declines, your asset declines and you lose.

8 Short option should bring minimum $0.50.

9 If there is a positive skew (sell minus buy) that is greater than 6, investigate. This is somewhat different from what some teach — that is, sell high-volatility near option against buying a lower-volatility far option. The bigger the skew, the bigger the anticipated move. "If you see a big skew, picture yourself on the beach in Florida a day before a hurricane is expected," Sheridan says. "That's your reality. Do you *really* want to be there?" If there is more than a skew of 6, he suggests asking why. And probably avoid that trade.

Place the trade

1 As a limit order at midpoints of buy and sell

2 Wait five minutes. If you don't get it, give in a nickel, no more.

Manage the trade

1 99% of being successful is risk management.

2 For risk management points — that is, breakeven points — place your adjustment orders in advance. At the very least, have your adjustment plan *in writing* in advance. Sheridan usually adjusts calendars by adding another calendar one strike up or down.

Pain avoidance

How do you get hurt with a calendar spread? There are two ways:

1 If volatility goes down, *or*

2 Stock moves big, up or down, thus squeezing the values of the short and long options together.

For the first, pick options that are low in their implied volatility range. For the second, avoid selling months where news can make the stock move — for example, earnings. Sheridan says that 99% of the time when there is a big move, it is earnings-related. Since you can control the timing of your trade, stay out of the period that can whack you with change.

Adjustments

If something can go wrong, it will. If the spread moves against you, what can you do?

1 On the upside, volumes come down, put another calendar spread on, higher strikes *or*

2 Take your short strike and roll up *or*

3 Close the trade. Sheridan notes that the structure of the calendar spread is such that even a fairly sizable move creates only small losses. In a larger move, the worst case is quantified at the initial debit. If you put a calendar spread on for $0.40, say, that's the most you can lose.

What about using a LEAP for the anchor, long option versus two or three months out? "The farther out, the more demanding I am on volatility," Sheridan says, meaning he wants lower and lower volatility for the LEAP anchor. "If you're long a LEAP and volatility declines, it can make a grown man cry," he quips.

Calls vs. puts

Should the strategist use calls or puts in a calendar? Calls trade more, so Sheridan tends to favor calls.

Case study: The guerrilla calendar

In Sheridan's FIA seminar, he showed his personal variation on the calendar theme: a "guerrilla" or one-month calendar spread example. (See sidebar, "Trader Dan on guerrilla calendars," for details.) He used Bank of New York (BK) as his example (Figure 1). On October 26, he:

Sold 10 December 35 calls	0.79
Bought 10 January 35 calls	1.10

Net debit: $0.31, plus $20 commissions = $330. If BK went to $1 million or zero the next day, the most Sheridan could lose would be $330.

What happened next? BK did *not* go to $1 million, nor did it

FIGURE 1: GUERRILLA CALENDAR. On October 26, 2006, Sheridan sold 10 December 35 calls and bought 10 January 35 calls. The net debit on this position was $330.

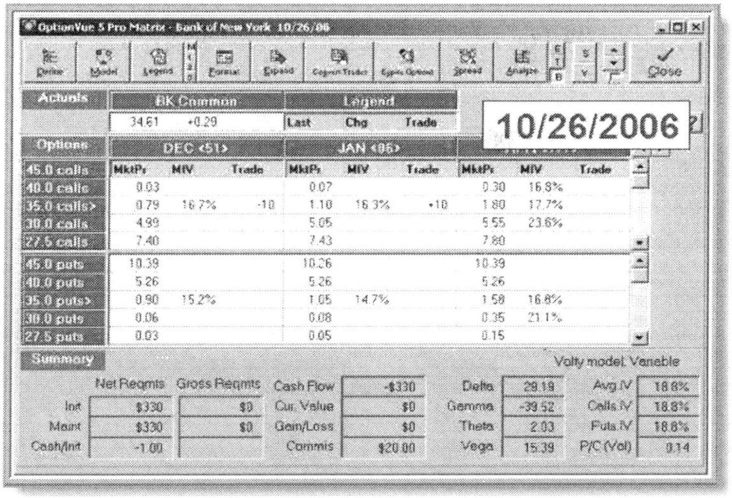

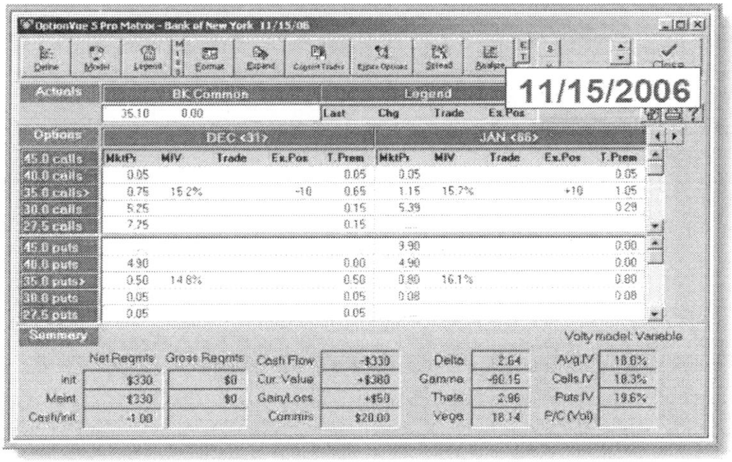

FIGURE 2: WHAT HAPPENED NEXT? BK went from 34.61 to 35.10 in the next 20 days. The trade was offset by buying 10 December 35 calls and selling 10 January 35 calls.

Should the strategist use calls or puts in a calendar? Calls trade more, so Sheridan tends to favor calls.

go to zero; instead, it went from $34.61 to $35.10 in the next 20 days, and Sheridan offset the trade:

Bought 10 December 35 calls   0.75
Sold 10 January 35 calls   1.15

Net credit: 0.40 minus $20 commissions = $380 net credit, $50 profit (Figure 2). Yield: 15.15% in 20 days. Small in dollars, yes, but large in yield, and Sheridan says there's plenty of time later to trade larger when you learn the craft.

John A. Sarkett is the developer of Option Wizard Scan and Scan Wizard software (http://option-wizard.com).

S&C

11

PATRICK KELLEY

Strategies From Trader Dan (Part 2)

Double Calendars And Condors

In this, the second part of a series based on an option seminar with trader Dan Sheridan, we look at the double calendar and condor strategies.

---

by John A. Sarkett

With a stock at 50, an option strategist could put on a call calendar at 55 and a put calendar at 45, short June, long November, hence creating a "double calendar." Is this a good vehicle? Trader Dan Sheridan is ambivalent: "I'd rather put the calendar right at 50 and make the stock prove it's going to move, and then adjust by putting on another calendar at a higher or lower level."

A "better" double calendar, in Sheridan's opinion, is an *adjusted* single calendar. If the stock moves up to 55, sell the July 55 calls, buy the November 55 calls. The risk curve changes to look like the chart in Figure 1.

DOUBLE CALENDARS
Double calendars work best in a low-volatility environment. (Double diagonals work in both low- and high-volatility environments.) If the strategist turns bullish, a calendar can also be adjusted into a diagonal. In the case study used as an example in this article, with HDI moving up to 50.93, a strategist adjusts by selling his June 50 call and buying the November 50 call, while staying short the June 55 call (Figure 2). This forces the stock to move to 55 before profit

OPTIONS

decline sets in. The risk curve then looks like what you see in Figure 3.

CONDORS

An *iron condor* is two credit spreads, a call credit spread above the market and a put credit spread below. (A credit spread is where you buy one option and sell another, and receive money or a "credit." A debit spread is where you buy one option and sell another and pay money to do it.)

Other condors can be constructed of just puts or just calls, but mixing calls and puts makes this one an "iron" condor. The risk is limited to the amount between the two strikes, typically 10 points minus the credit received.

But do you have to suffer the full 10-point loss after you get your credit, typically $1 to $1.50? No, you can *adjust* during the trade. As Sheridan says, "Doesn't matter what happens in the market, if you have a plan, you'll be fine."

CHOOSING TIMES, STRIKES

Dan Sheridan likes to initiate an index condor 49 days before expiration, and ideally get out one to two weeks before expiration. (See sidebar "Trader Dan on index condors.") He looks to place the trade one standard deviation away from market. It would take a major market move to hit your short options, an improbability. So you start the trade with the odds in your favor. His software of choice, OptionVue, calculates the standard deviation in the matrix. Strikes and their options within one standard deviation are backdropped in purple, and two standard deviations are highlighted in aqua. Sheridan sells the option at the outer range of one standard deviation far away, and buys the next option farther away, one strike into the next standard deviation.

His short calls typically have a delta of 7 to 8, and his short puts have a delta of 6 to 7. (His put credit spread is typically one more strike away from the market than the call side because stocks go down much faster than they go up, so this gives him extra room. For this reason, Sheridan calls the condor a "collie that can suddenly turn into a pit bull" — hence, the extra room on the downside.)

Because index options don't trade at six exchanges, just one, and because it's harder to get the middle price of the spread due to

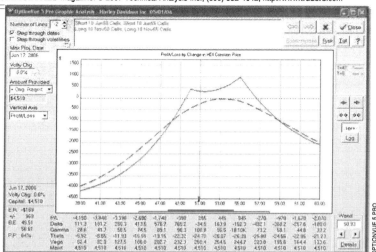

FIGURE 1: DOUBLE CALENDAR. Here you see the risk curve of an adjusted single calendar, which can provide better results than the traditional double calendar.

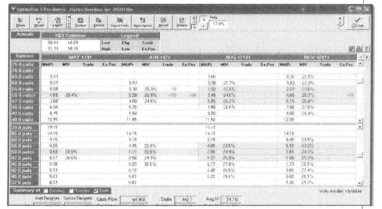

FIGURE 2: THE DIAGONAL. If you are bullish, a calendar can be adjusted into a diagonal. Here, when the price of the stock moves up to 50.93, you adjust by selling the June 50 call and buying the November 50 call while staying short the June 55 call. See Figure 3 for the resulting risk curve.

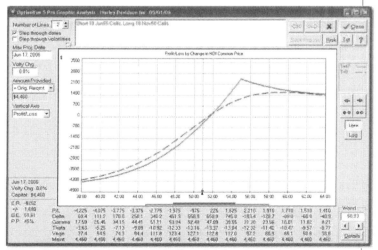

FIGURE 3: PROFIT/LOSS BY CHANGE IN PRICE. The profit declines after the price hits 55.

the lack of competition, Sheridan says that he will leg into the spread.

THE BIG 4 RULES OF ADJUSTMENTS

Here's how Dan Sheridan manages the trade. He adjusts the trade when:

1 Delta on the short call reaches 25, rising from a start of 7 to 8. This is often within 10 points of the strike.

2 Delta on the short put reaches 20, from 6 to 7. Again, this is often within 10 points of the strike.

3 Credit spread can be offset for 0.20 or less. "Take off the risk," Sheridan says.

4 He can lock up 50% to 60% of his net credit as a gain for the trade.

CASE STUDY

Let's follow a real trade to see how this plays out in the real world. On September 29, 2006, with the Russell 1000 index at 725.60, Dan Sheridan initiated this condor with 49 days to go to the November 2006 expiration (Figure 4):

Sell 10 800 calls	1.40
Buy 10 810 calls	0.85
Credit:	*0.55*

Sell 10 640 puts	3.30
Buy 10 630 puts	2.60
Credit:	*0.70*

Total credit, calls and puts = 1.35

After commissions, this generates a cash flow credit of $1,210. The risk curve of this condor can be seen in Figure 5. By October 12 — 13 days later — the market has moved up, from 725 to 757, and one of Dan Sheridan's rules of adjustment has been triggered: the put credit spread can be offset for 0.20. He does so to remove the risk:

Buy 10 640 puts	0.65
Sell 10 630 puts	0.45
Debit:	*0.20*

At the same time, he replaces it higher:

Sell 10 690 puts	2.50
Buy 10 680 puts	1.90
Credit:	*0.60*

Over the next 19 days, the market has moved a sum total of five points higher, and Sheridan is able to take off both sides of the trade at 0.20 — 19 days before expiration:

Close out the trade	
Buy 10 690 puts	0.50

FIGURE 4: A CONDOR IN THE REAL WORLD. The Russell 1000 (RUT) is at 725.60 when this condor is initiated. There are 49 days till the November 2006 expiration.

Credit spread can be offset for 0.20 or less. "Take off the risk," Sheridan says.

Sell 10 680 puts	0.30
Net debit:	*0.20*

Buy 10 800 calls	0.50
Sell 10 810 calls	0.30
Net debit:	*0.20*

With only one adjustment, as the market moved higher, Sheridan generated $1,130 of profit on $8,890 margin from September 29 to November 1, 2006 — 32 days, a yield of 12.7%.

This is a relatively benign example, requiring only one adjustment. What about when things turn ugly? In his Futures Industry Association webinar, Dan Sheridan worked through the May 2006 Russell 1000 condor, the worst month in five years, he says, and showed how two (his maximum number) timely adjustments generated a gain of $1,900 (minus another $440 in commissions) on $10,000 risk, or a 14.6% yield on

---

TRADER DAN ON INDEX CONDORS

- Put on five to seven weeks from expiration (preferably 49 days for new students)
- Strike width: Five to 20 points in SPX & RUT; NDX 25 to 50 points
- Strike width: One to five points in DIA, SPY, IWM
- Low-probability condors, don't look at deltas to adjust to take off
- Minimum credits: $0.35 side five-point strikes, $0.50 credit 10-point strikes, $0.75 credit 20- to 25-point strikes
- Sell call option between seven and nine delta
- Sell put option between six and seven delta

TRADER DAN'S DAILY CONDOR CHECKLIST

1. Has call short delta hit around 22–25 or put 20–22? Take off bad spread. Wait 24–48 hours and roll both spreads up on upside and down on downside.

2. Never add new short calls over 10 deltas on calls or puts!

3. Have credit spreads shrunk to $0.15–$0.20? Take off.

4. Have profits hit 50%–60% of cash flow? If yes, "tighten noose" — that is, change your adjustment points from breakeven to profit-protect, ignore delta.

5. Has loss hit one or one and a half times cash flow? That is the most you should let the condor lose. Take it off, come back to play another day.

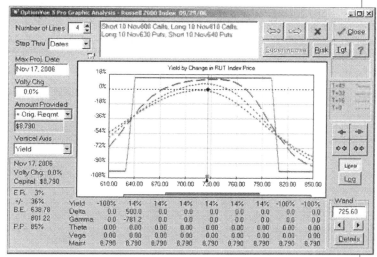

FIGURE 5: RISK CURVE OF CONDOR

margin funds required. The key is risk management, he explains.

Alternately, if Sheridan forecasts that the market will calm down and move sideways again, he will also increase size by 50% on the adjustment to generate more cash flow to make up for losses to date. It's also important to note when calculating the new standard deviation to determine repositioning points — that is, points where you sell and buy new strikes — to use the implied volatility of the ATM call option.

John A. Sarkett is the developer of Option Wizard Scan and Scan Wizard software (http://option-wizard.com).

SUGGESTED READING

Sarkett, John A. [2007] "Calendar Spreads With Dan Sheridan," *Technical Analysis of* STOCKS & COMMODITIES, Volume 25: May.

S&C

TIM FOLEY

Trading With Dan Sheridan (Part 3)

Double Diagonals And Butterfly Spreads

The third part of this series with trader Dan Sheridan looks at double diagonals with long, protective wings one or more months out from the short options, as well as the butterfly spread, an income-generating strategy.

by John A. Sarkett

ouble diagonals are Dan Sheridan's single favorite strategy, and he likes to mix double diagonals in a portfolio with condors for diversification. Here's why: While increasing volatilities hurts the condors, it *helps* the diagonals. So one offsets the other. Let's look at double diagonals first.

DOUBLE DIAGONALS

In addition, the double diagonals strategy has a more favorable risk–reward ratio than other income strategies — 1:2, 1:3, 1:4, compared with 1:10 for condors. The yields can reach 15% to 30% for 30 days on average.

Remember, this is a business — "An insurance company without the overhead," as Sheridan says. Remember, he was a market maker for 22 years. Everything he does is hedged, quantified, managed, and managed in advance, "managed in times of peace, not in times of war," as he puts it.

Best option candidates for double diagonal strategy

■ Stock is greater than $30

- Implied volatility (IV) in lowest two thirds of its two-year range
- Nontrenders, sideways movers
- Low volatilities (for nonmovers, we want to go sideways)
- Skews (volatilities near and far) in line, not more than four points apart
- Nonearnings months — again, we don't want movement due to news
- Boring, sideways, predictable industries, no biotech startups or the like.

Filter

1 Sell the call option strike (minimum 0.50 for short option) in the front month that is the first strike inside one standard deviation.

2 Sell the put option strike (minimum 0.50 for short option) in the front month that is the first strike inside one standard deviation.

3 Buy call one to two months out from short option and up one strike (maximum one and a half times the price of a short call).

4 Buy put one to two months out from short option and down one strike (maximum one and a half times the price of a short option).

5 If the profit/loss graph sags in the middle, then bring the short and long options in one strike.

6 If a negative skew of greater than 2 exists (long month minus short month), then don't do the trade!

7 If a positive skew of 4 or more exists, then investigate.

8 Know the earnings date and past gap potential.

Case study

Here's a double-diagonal example that Sheridan gave his option seminar session-goers. On October 13, 2006, with Whirlpool (WHR) at $88.83, Sheridan:

> Sold 10 Nov 95 calls
> Bought 10 Dec 100 calls
>
> Sold 10 Nov 80 puts
> Bought 10 Dec 75 puts
>
> Credit: $0.73 or $730
> Risk: $5,000

The plan

Dan Sheridan's strategy is:

1 Adjustment target points were set at Whirlpool 81 and 94. This is where the risk curve showed losses gathering speed. If Whirlpool hits 81 or 94, roll the credits.

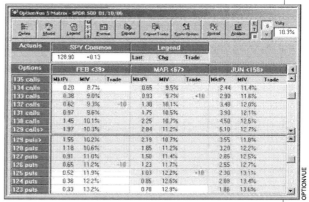

FIGURE 1: THE DOUBLE DIAGONAL. When your long option is greater than one and a half times your short position, you have a poor profit prospect.

2 When either credit can be taken off for less than 0.20, do it.

3 When half of the initial cash flow can be closed out as profit, do it.

MANAGING THE TRADE

As time goes on, the adjustment target points are brought in closer and closer to the market; instead of protecting breakevens, you are now protecting profits. Sheridan calls this "tightening the noose." After 15 days, the risk curve shows that yield on the strategy drops after Whirlpool (WHR) hits 84.50 on the downside, or 91.50 on the upside, so these become the new adjustment points.

Another rule of thumb: Adjust at half the distance between the short strike and breakeven. If you are expecting the trend to abate, roll up (or down) your short strike — that is, buy in your short option and resell it higher (for example, in short 55 near month, sell 60 call next month out).

If neutral, Sheridan adjusts by turning the double-diagonal trade into a neutral calendar spread (buy in short 55 call near month, sell 55 call next month out). If an adjustment cannot improve the risk curve of the trade, he takes it off and moves on to the next opportunity. He doesn't nurse a losing position — ever: "I'm not just *hoping* to make money every month. This is a business. I have a *plan* to make money," he states.

On the November 17th expiration, WHR was 86.50. The whole net credit spread premium was captured, and the strategist still held the wings — that is, the December 100 calls and the December 75 puts.

Major caveats

Here are some things to watch out for. Beware when:

While increasing volatilities hurts the condors, it helps the diagonals. So one offsets the other.

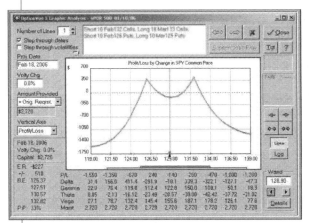

FIGURE 2: SAGGY BOTTOM. This is what happens when your long option is greater than one and a half times your short option.

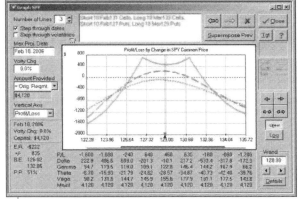

FIGURE 4: THE "SAGGY" BOTTOM TIGHTENS

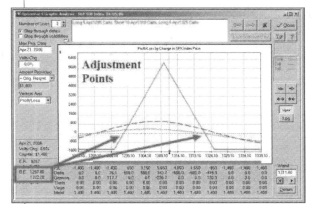

FIGURE 5: THE INCOME BUTTERFLY. Adjust points on an income butterfly can be seen where the profit/loss points cross zero on the graph. Different lines represent different points in time. When a trade starts to lose money, Dan Sheridan adjusts the trade by buying in the losing side, and placing the trade out further.

Actuals	SPY Common		Legend		
	128.90	+0.13	Last	Chg	Trade
Options	**FEB <39>**		**MAR <67>**		
135 calls	MktPr	MIV	Trade	MktPr	MIV	Trade
134 calls	0.20	8.7%		0.65	9.5%	
133 calls	0.38	9.0%		0.93	9.7%	+10
132 calls	0.62	9.3%		1.30	10.1%	
131 calls	0.97	9.6%	–10	1.75	10.5%	
130 calls	1.45	10.1%		2.25	10.7%	
129 calls>	1.97	10.3%		2.84	11.2%	
129 puts>	1.55	10.2%		2.19	10.7%	
128 puts	1.18	10.6%		1.85	11.2%	
127 puts	0.91	11.0%	–10	1.50	11.4%	
126 puts	0.65	11.2%		1.23	11.7%	
125 puts	0.52	11.9%		1.03	12.2%	+10
124 puts	0.38	12.2%		0.85	12.6%	
123 puts	0.33	13.2%		0.70	12.9%	

FIGURE 3: SELL LOWER CALLS AND HIGHER PUTS. Here, the 127s and 131s are sold instead of the 126 and 132 to improve the profit-loss graph.

- Your long option is greater than one and a half times your short option (Figure 1). This will make for a "saggy bottom" in the risk curve, a poor profit prospect (Figure 2).

- You are paying too much. To fix this, go back and sell lower calls and higher puts to generate more income. In Figure 3, the strategist sells the 127s and 131s versus the 126 and 132 to create a better profit-loss graph.

And voilà, the "saggy bottom" tightens (Figure 4).

You should not put double diagonals on during earnings months. There is too great a prospect for a major move that could turn a winner into a loser in one day.

What can you do when the stock gaps beyond the short strike? Close the position. "I don't play games with these things," Sheridan says.

Suppose a double diagonal is put on and the stock doesn't meander sideways as was hoped, but moves a strong 5% up or down within the first few days? Dan Sheridan advises getting out at a small loss, with consideration toward repositioning the trade at a different level a week or so later if the situation warrants it.

BUTTERFLY SPREADS

A short (or income) butterfly is selling two at-the-money (ATM) calls, buying one call under and one call over, as in the following example. Viewed on a monthly basis, it is a high-yield vehicle (Figure 5).

Dan Sheridan's income butterfly management checklist

1 Pick a low-volatility stock. Sheridan's tip: The time after earnings news has been digested is typically a quiet, low IV time, and a good time to put on a butterfly.

2 A tactic for butterflies is to put on with four weeks before expiration and "tighten the noose" or take off at about two weeks before expiration. "Tighten the noose" refers to setting adjustment points closer and closer to the market to profit profits, as more and more time is logged in the trade.

3 Maximum loss: Around a quarter to a third of what you paid for the butterfly.

4 Buy butterfly 25 to 35 days till expiration.

5 Sell ATM strikes and buy long positions five to 50 points away, depending on the vehicle.

6 Set adjustment points at breakevens (BEs) at expiration plus 1.5% of underlying for extra room (first two weeks) (1.5% of 72.50 for IWM = 1.0875). Easiest way to see the breakevens is to review the risk curve.

7 Tighten the adjustment points to BEs for the last two weeks.

8 Tighten noose when up 20% on (at this point, have stop orders in no lower than 10% yields to take off).

9 For OptionVue users, set slippage on small to moderate when deciding when to get out.

10 At all costs, try to be out by Friday before expiration.

11 Butterfly candidates:
- MDY: 10-point strikes
- IWM: Five-point strikes
- SML: 25-point strikes
- MID: 30–40 point strikes

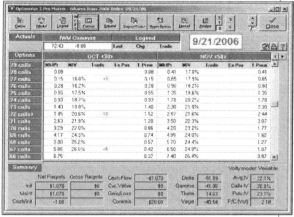

FIGURE 6: INCOME BUTTERFLY IN ACTION. Here's an example using iShares of the Russell 2000 index.

- RUT: 50-point strikes
- SPY: Five-point strikes

12 Be patient when putting on a trade. Use midprices and cave in 0.05 if necessary.

13 As Dan Sheridan says: "Once you get more familiar trading butterflies, your acceptable losses will be based on what profits you're taking out of butterflies in the good months. For example, if you find yourself taking 20% profits of $600 consistently and not going for more, then maximum loss would be around $600."

TRADER DAN ON OPTIONS ADJUSTMENT

An "adjustment" is changing your trade as the market changes. You don't have to do it every month if you're selling at the edge of standard deviation from the underlying, the way Dan Sheridan does, but you have to do it, at least if you want to treat options as a business and not as a gamble.

"Adjusting" is a peculiar advantage to the option market, unlike straight-up futures or stock trading where stop-losses and stop limits create gains or losses. Option adjustments allow you to put the trade on again, often for another credit offsetting a loss taken at the same time and giving yourself more time for option decay to work for you. Adjustments can be closing:

- One part of a trade and putting it on again at a higher or lower level — that is, "rolling," *or*
- One leg of a trade out, *or*
- The entire trade out.

Dan Sheridan's general rules of adjustment include:

1 Pocket 50%. If your paper gain is greater than 50% of your initial, take the trade off. Look elsewhere for your next profit opportunity.

2 20-cent rule. If one of the credit spreads on a delta neutral strategy (condors, butterflies, double diagonals) can be removed for $0.20 or less, take it off.

3 20 delta rule. If delta has shot up to be greater than 20 on a sold option, take that side off. Roll it to a strike where delta is 3-7 again.

4 1.5 x cash flow rule. Hard and fast rule: Never lose more than one and a half times your cash flow. If your paper loss is one and a half times your credit, take it off and take the loss.

5 15-day rule. If you must adjust within 15 days of expiration, close the trade. You are too short of time, there is too little theta vis-à-vis too much potential delta, or movement, and hence too much risk in the trade.

6 Two-roll rule. Roll down at most two times. If more is required, then "forces bigger than me are at work, and I'll stand aside," Dan Sheridan says.

7 Adjustment cash. Keep 10% of your trading account in cash for adjustments.

OFF THE BEATEN TRACK: Q&A WITH TRADER DAN

Q. Why do calendars and butterflies, why not just buy puts and calls? Or better, why not just sell naked options?

Dan Sheridan: Because over time, you'll lose. You'll get your ears ripped off. You want to put the odds in your favor, and you want to manage risk, if you're serious about being in the options business over time.

Q. How do you handle assignments?

Dan Sheridan: Most of the time when an option goes in the money, we have adjusted before that time, so we are not facing assignment. On those rare occasions we do get assigned, we are protected by the opposite option transaction.

Q. Do you enter condors, calendars, and butterflies as spread orders, or do you leg in?

Dan Sheridan: Most times we will leg in. I know this is contrary to what many teach. But as a market maker, I know you will stand a better chance of getting better prices for your spread by putting it together as component parts than as a complete spread. Price your option in the middle of the bid and ask, and cave in a nickel and no more. Here's the problem with spread orders. If you have a good idea and send it to the market, many times the market maker will look at it, say "Good idea. I'd like to do it, too," and put it on the bottom of the stack where it will gather dust. Index spreads are not traded at six markets like equity options (AMEX, BOX, CBOE, ISE, PHLX, PSE); there is a lack of competition to fill your order.

Q. I've been taught to sell high volatility and buy low volatility, as a rule. Is this correct?

Dan Sheridan: No! High volatility means there is a

tornado in the air. The market is saying something is going to happen, trust the market. When trading spreads, buy and sell volumes that are in line. If the difference between options is more than six points, investigate, or — since life is short — just look elsewhere.

Q. What is the "weekend theta drop"?

Dan Sheridan: Retail customers think they'll come in the market on Friday and sell the options and pick up two days of theta for free. Market makers are onto this. As market makers, we used to start lowering volatilities to cover this Friday mornings. So be aware.

Q. What's the single most important thing to keep in mind when trading options?

Dan Sheridan: That's easy. Have a risk management plan. Be prepared for the position to move against you, don't be bushwacked by it and sit there frozen in the headlights like Bambi. Know your adjustment points on each and every trade when you put on the trade. Have your contingency orders in the market immediately after your trade is filled. Make it a business, not a speculation. None of this "I'm going to watch it, or I'm going to take the pain." Do your planning in times of peace, not in times of war. If you do that, you'll do well over time.

Q. Any special thoughts on brokers?

Dan Sheridan: I recommend brokers who can take contingency orders, offer spread order capability, and charge $1 per contract or less. These are typically the options brokerage specialists, and there are some four or five of these in the market at the present time.

Case study

Here's an example using iShares of the Russell 2000 index (IWM) (see Figure 6). On September 21, 2006, Dan Sheridan:

> Bought five 67 calls
> Sold 10 72 calls
> Bought five 77 calls

The total debit was $1,070.

The longer the market stays around the center strike — for example, for IWM, 72 — the more profitable the trade becomes. The risk curve of this trade is displayed in Figure 7.

Sticking with his discipline to be *out* of the trade two weeks before expiration, Sheridan was able to generate a 17% return on invested capital from September 29 to October 11 (20 days). (See Figure 8.)

It is important to note that IWM closed on October 20, 2006 (expiration), at 75.60. Had Dan Sheridan sat on the trade he

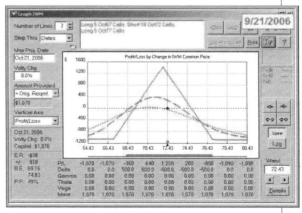

FIGURE 7: RISK CURVE OF THE INCOME BUTTERFLY. The longer the market stays around the center strike, the more profitable the trade becomes.

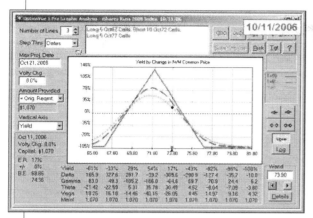

FIGURE 8: THE CLOSER TO EXPIRATION, THE GREATER THE RISK. Since the trade was closed two weeks before expiration, Sheridan was able to generate a 17% return from September 29, 2006, to October 11, 2006.

would have lost, as the risk curve shows. The closer the option is to expiration, the greater the risk. Sheridan manages risk. When he can avoid it altogether, he does so.

SPECULATIVE BUTTERFLIES

Dan Sheridan calls speculative butterflies "time bombs." For a very small investment, a high risk-reward profile can be generated. Put these on before earnings; high volatilities are acceptable. In this case (Figure 9), Sheridan:

> Sells two 1280 puts, 2.54 each, total 5.08
>
> Buys the 1295 put, 4.89
>
> Buys the 1265 put, 1.24
>
> Net debit: $1.05

The profit-loss curve looks like what you see in Figure 10. A $1,050 investment in this bearish strategy could return as much as $14,000, a 1:13.3 risk–reward ratio.

John Sarkett is the designer of Option Wizard Scan (options) and Scan Wizard (stocks) software and writes about financial markets and other topics. His new book, Extraordinary Comebacks, *includes chapters on business and finance.*

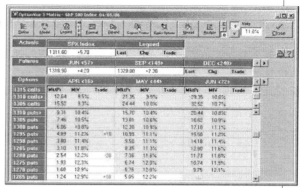

FIGURE 9: SPECULATIVE BUTTERFLY. Dan Sheridan refers to these as "time bombs."

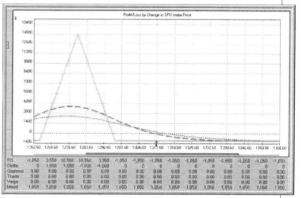

FIGURE 10: PROFIT-LOSS CURVE OF THE SPECULATIVE BUTTERFLY. The profit-loss curve looks like this.

SUGGESTED READING

Sarkett, John A. [2007]. *Extraordinary Comebacks: 201 Inspiring Stories Of Courage, Triumph, and Success,* Sourcebooks.
• http://option-wizard.com
• www.cboe.com/LearnCenter/webcast/archive.aspx

S&C

DAN HARVEY:
The Supertrader Of Index Condors

Dan Harvey, 62 years old, is an independent, full-time and successful trader of delta-neutral strategies. His specialty is with index condors. It's not too great an exaggeration to say that what Michael Jordan was to basketball, Harvey is to condor trading—except for the fact that Jordan worked his magic in public, while Harvey is known to only a few.

By John A. Sarkett

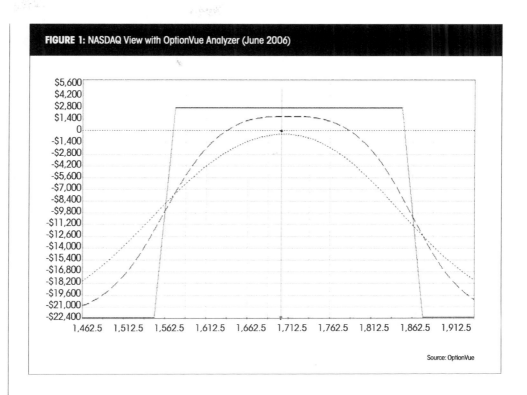

FIGURE 1: NASDAQ View with OptionVue Analyzer (June 2006)

Source: OptionVue

Harvey has all the traits of the master trader: He is organized, decisive, humble (he has a distinguished scientific background but never mentions it), yet is open-minded and always ready to learn—even after 14 successful years. That's why he joined the Sheridan Mentoring community, to learn from another Dan—Dan Sheridan—and to polish his skills. As a result, Harvey was well rewarded. As good as he was, Harvey managed to increase his monthly returns from 1 percent to 2 percent, all the way up to 3 percent to 5 percent (and as high as 6 percent monthly when figured on risk capital alone, or 10 percent to 12 percent monthly when figured on portfolio margin), which is a testimony to Sheridan's expertise and teaching ability. Recalling the line from Walt Whitman's *Song of Myself*: "He who by me spreads a wider breast than my own proves the width of my own." (Sheridan forged his expertise for some 22 years in the foundry of the CBOE pits, trading literally millions of contracts. He presently has some 500 students, 3,000 webinars and is widely regarded by the cognoscenti as the No. 1 options mentor.)

Soon enough, Harvey was called on by Sheridan to occasionally teach others at CBOE seminars and online via webinars. Hence, Sheridan Mentoring students are receiving the benefit of Dan squared.

What do the two Dans teach? In a word: adjustment. For them, trading options is virtually the same as making adjustments. That is their methodology—their edge, if you will. And with 14 years of success under Harvey's belt, adjusting an options trade is (almost) as natural and unthinking as breathing. (Only one out of the 168 months of delta-neutral condor trading has Harvey made no adjustments.)

Adjustment can take a trade that would otherwise lose big and carve out a small profit, sometimes a large profit or a breakeven. It gives the trader market stamina, the ability to stay in the market and earn profits over time, instead of, like many, blowing up and unfortunately blowing away.

LEARN BY EXAMPLE

The best way to learn Harvey's condor method is to work through an example with

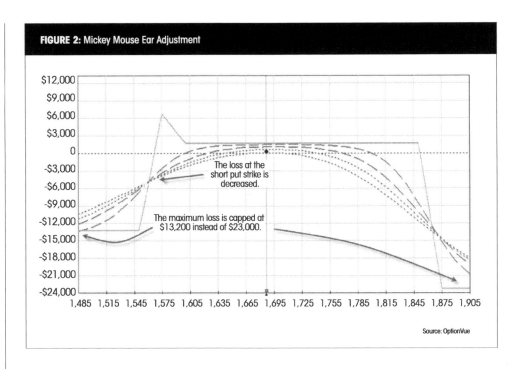

FIGURE 2: Mickey Mouse Ear Adjustment

The loss at the short put strike is decreased.

The maximum loss is capped at $13,200 instead of $23,000.

Source: OptionVue

him, to which he graciously agreed. Harvey picked one of the worst scenarios in recent times—the June 2006 plummet of the NAS-DAQ-100 Index (NDX)—to illustrate the power of timely adjustment.

The NDX can be a violent mover—50 to 100 points in a day, at times—but Harvey likes this vehicle for condors because the premiums are commensurately richer. However, less experienced traders are advised to start with less violent vehicles, such as the Russell 2000 Index, because their movements are smoother.

A condor is a simple enough vehicle: a call credit spread on top, a put credit spread on the bottom. What makes it challenging is the risk-reward ratio. It's terrible. So bad that it causes many traders to look at it once and never again. A trader typically risks 10 points to make $1 to $1.50. In this NDX example, a trader similarly risks 25 points to make $2.70. This surely runs contrary to the old saw in futures trading: risk $1 to make $3.

However, if the trader is smart and nimble enough to adjust as the trade evolves, he or she can manage those potentially catastrophic outcomes and turn them into a profit. It's quite an art; Harvey and his mentor, Sheridan, are artists.

Let's roll up our sleeves and get started by looking over Harvey's shoulder as he undertakes an NDX trade in the most severe and hostile climate he could find in recent years—the June 2006 expiration.

IN THE BEGINNING

On April 24, 2006, the NDX is in sideways action. Approximately 53 days in advance of expiration, it's time for Harvey to put his hook in the water—just like he does every month. He places a 1,550/1,575/1,850/1,875 condor, and he receives a $2.70 credit: $1.20 (call) and $1.50 (put) credit. For a 10 lot, that's $2,700 minus commissions. Deltas on the short strikes are 5.47 (calls) and -6.36 (puts), which is well within his guidelines of 7 to 8 for calls and -6 to -7 for puts.

Figure 1 is how it looks in the OptionVue Analyzer: A perfect start; the market is smack in the middle of the risk curve, right where it is supposed to be. "Take a good look," Harvey says, "it's not going to stay like this much longer." Unbeknownst to him at the time, the market was about to crater.

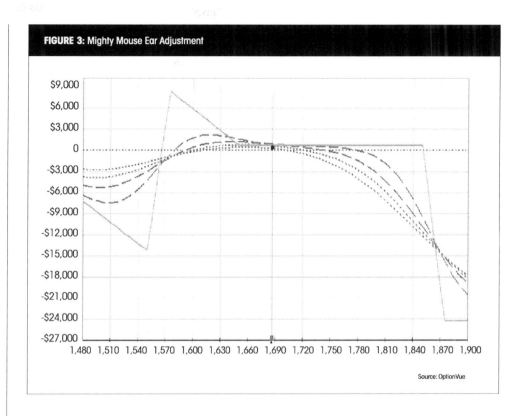

FIGURE 3: Mighty Mouse Ear Adjustment

Source: OptionVue

IN THE MIDST OF TRADING

Harvey offers a couple of guidelines to keep in mind while trading condors.

1. Trade condors as if they were naked strangles. He says, "Your concentration should always be on the short strike." The wings will contain loss and reduce margin, but that's all. The money will be made on the risk management of the short strikes.

2. Should a trader place contingent exit orders in the market for protection, especially with the potentially large losses a condor can incur? Harvey says it's a personal decision that requires a trader to weigh both advantages and disadvantages.

   Advantages:
   • Protection—especially if you're traveling or otherwise unable to follow the market through the day.
   • Automatic execution—no getting stuck in the headlights.

   Disadvantages:
   • A bad print (which is a reported transaction away from the market that may or may not have happened but "prints" to the trading screen and triggers stop losses) will take you out.
   • Not typically getting midprices (i.e., price between the bid and ask). Most contingent orders require "market" execution (i.e., buy at the ask; sell at the bid).

3. Establish your maximum loss. "You don't want to lose in one month what will take you four to five months to make back." Harvey suggests 1.5 times cash flow as a reasonable target. "It's a personal decision," he says. "It depends where you are in life, in your trading, etc., but the main thing is to determine your 'out' point. And do it in advance."

Additionally, Harvey mentions some adjustment possibilities that traders must consider:
• Do nothing (Harvey says this tongue-in-cheek): "If you have one or two contracts on, you could do nothing, and nine or 10 months per year, you would make all your credits," he says, but notes that you might give back all your gains and

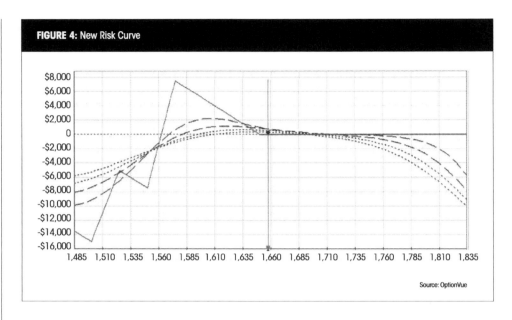

FIGURE 4: New Risk Curve

Source: OptionVue

perhaps even more on occasion as well. This is not recommended.

- Add various combinations of long options: Add long options, long debit spreads or calendars to cut risk, decrease delta and lower volatility risk. (These examples are visited later.)
- Cut and roll (Harvey's preferred method): He does this every month. "It's part of my game."

BACK TO THE MARKET

What happens next? The market plummets. By May 23, if Harvey had done nothing, delta on his short put would have ballooned to -50, and he would be down $7,800. But doing nothing is not Harvey's style. Here's what he actually did instead. The trigger was a technical analysis point. On May 1, the NDX breaks the 50-day moving average, alarms sound and Harvey moves to adjust. He considers several alternatives:

1. Mickey Mouse ear: Harvey considers adding a Mickey Mouse ear to the trade (i.e., a long put debit spread), placed at 1,600/1,550 but not for the entire 10 lot, just for two. When graphed, the put debit spread forms a small "ear," which is what gives the adjustment the name Mickey Mouse ear. What does this new adjustment do for the risk characteristics of the

trade? See Figure 2. Cost of adjustment: $970 ($9.75 - $4.90 x 200).

2. Embedded calendar: Harvey also considers an embedded calendar, aiming for two standard deviations out of the money. "If the market continues to move down, I'm going to be moving into the sweet spot of the calendar," he says. "If I reach the sweet spot [the middle], I'll take the profit and reposition it further out."

What if the market moves up?

"I'm going to have a stop loss in where I don't lose more than a couple hundred dollars." The net result: Harvey would cut deltas by half, add theta and decrease the short vega. Cost: $28.90 - $19.90 = $9 x 200 = $1,800, about twice as much.

3. Mighty Mouse ear (also called the "Silver Bullet"): Simple enough, this is buying one put (against a 10 x 10 put credit spread), two to three strikes in front of the short strike. This makes a risk curve with a bigger ear, vis-à-vis the put debit spread, hence the name Mighty Mouse (see Figure 3).

At $19.90 x 100 (a one lot), or $1,990, the Mighty Mouse ear is the most expensive adjustment on the table so far. Although he would get increased protection on the downside, a market reversal would be costly. Harvey advises a sale on a market rally, so

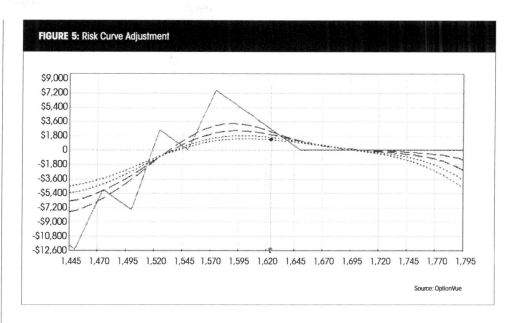

FIGURE 5: Risk Curve Adjustment

Source: OptionVue

it requires vigilance. "Everything comes at a cost in options," Harvey says. "Everything is a tradeoff."

Which will it be: Mickey Mouse, calendar or Mighty Mouse? Harvey chooses the Mighty Mouse ear in this situation because the market was dropping so violently. But under normal circumstances, he says he would go first with an embedded calendar, then add a Mighty Mouse ear if the market suddenly dropped.

MEANWHILE ...

By May 4, the market is moving slightly higher; if it continues, long put (Mighty Mouse) will be sold at a small loss. But by May 11, the market is heading south again. Mighty Mouse is paying for himself—"Here he comes to save the day," as the song goes. Again triggered by technical analysis, the NDX trendline and 50-day moving average are both violated, so he cuts and rolls. But here is where the artistry comes into play. Instead of the entire position, Harvey cuts just three of the original 10 put spreads and then replaces them with a five lot at an approximate -5 delta. Condor management requires adding size when rolling, hence the buying of three spreads and the sale of five more. Figure 4 shows what the new risk curve looks like.

One week later, at 1,623, the NDX is losing ground again. The short strike delta is -22, and Harvey determines he must adjust once more. He buys three of the remaining original seven put spreads and resells four at 1,475/1,450. Figure 5 shows what the risk curve now looks like.

"The Mighty Mouse ear is kicking in," Harvey says. "And we're still in control." Just one day later, that control is sorely tested when the NDX plummets 24 points. "We are very glad we have the Mighty Mouse ear here," Harvey notes. With delta at -32, he decides to offset the remaining four original put spreads and sell five to replace these farther out at 1,475/1,450.

Harvey comments: "We're still OK, but our chance of profit is diminishing if we don't reach a bottom soon."

On May 30, the NDX falls 35 points, but the trade is up $1,131. Why? The Mighty Mouse ear. "[This is] because the 1,650 put premium is now $81.60 [bought at $19.90] and because theta is increasing," Harvey explains.

This is when the situation gets truly interesting: the end game. As Harvey says, "Here's the art of trading! On June 2, NDX has increased to 1,613—88 away from the short put. Do we sell our ear?" It's a personal decision based on forecast Harvey says.

FIGURE 6: Profits from Adjustment

Posn Type	Underly Symbol	Desc	Type	Open Date	Close Date	Posn	Open Price	Close Price	Commis on Open	Commis on Close	Total Commis	Open Cost (Proceeds)	Close Proceeds (Cost)	Gain (Loss)
Comb	NDX	NDX Jun 1550 puts	O	4/24/06	5/11/06	+3								
	NDX	NDX Jun 1575 puts	O	4/24/06	5/11/06	-3								
	NDX	NDX Jun 1550 puts	O	4/26/06	5/16/06	+3								
	NDX	NDX Jun 1575 puts	O	4/26/06	5/16/06	-3								
	NDX	NDX Jun 1550 puts	O	4/26/06	5/17/06	+4								
	NDX	NDX Jun 1575 puts	O	4/26/06	5/17/06	-4								
	NDX	NDX Jun 1850 calls	O	4/26/06	6/9/06	-10								
	NDX	NDX Jun 1875 calls	O	4/26/06	6/9/06	+10	$5.70	$12.85	$4	$8	$12	($2,696)	($4,178)	($1,482)
Comb	NDX	NDX Jun 1500 puts	O	5/11/06	6/9/06	+5								
	NDX	NDX Jun 1525 puts	O	5/11/06	6/9/06	-5								
	NDX	NDX Jun 1650 put	O	5/11/06	6/9/06	+1	$23.45	$95.65	$3	$3	$6	$2,028	$7,502	$5,474
Sprd	NDX	NDX Jun 1450 puts	O	5/16/06	6/9/06	+9								
	NDX	NDX Jun 1475 puts	O	5/16/06	6/9/06	-9	$0.95	$1	$4	$2	$6	($851)	($902)	$51
Totals									**Commissions: $24**				**Gain/Loss: $3,941**	

Slippage set to none.
Real commission rates were approximately $90.

Net profit approximately $3,900.

Source: OptionVue

He decides to wait watchfully. On June 6, NDX has fallen back to 1,575, but the position graph is improving because time is passing and options decay (theta) is accruing to his account.

On June 9, with seven days remaining, delta and gamma risk increasing, and profit in hand, Harvey says, "Let's vamoose. Let's take our money. We will close all positions, although the call spread—so far away at 1,850/1,875 while the NDX is 1,567.90—could be left in place."

The NDX on June 9 was 1,567.90. Had nothing been done, the short strike was in the money by 7.1 points—this vis-à-vis the original 2.3 credit. So there would have been a loss of approximately five points (or $5,000) by this time. Instead, through the skill of the trader, he earns a gain (see Figure 6).

ADVERSE CONDITIONS OVERCOME

Always a prospectively violent mover, NDX has, true to form, rocketed down from 1,706 to 1,567—a 9 percent decline from April 24 to June 9, but with a series of adjustments and largely thanks to the Mighty Mouse ear that made $7,502 all by itself, Harvey managed to generate a $3,941 profit on risk capital that could range from $22,304 (Reg T) to as low as $7,500 (portfolio margin)—for a yield of 17.7 percent (Reg T) to 52.5 percent (portfolio margin) from April 24 to June 9.

Whether the market soars or dives, for master trader Dan Harvey, or options mentor Dan Sheridan, in the final analysis, it really does not matter. The art—and the ultimate profit—is all in the adjustment.

John A. Sarkett writes frequently for SFO and other financial publications. He is the creator of Option Wizard® software (http://option-wizard.com) and author of the best-selling *Extraordinary Comebacks: 201 Inspiring Stories of Courage, Triumph, and Success.*

INTERVIEW

The Importance Of A Good Mentor

Adjusting Option Trades With Bill Ladd

Bill Ladd, a full-time, independent option trader, spent 20-some years in the pharmaceutical industry (Burroughs Wellcome, which became Glaxo Smith/Kline) as a certified internal auditor and a certified fraud examiner. Ladd was one of the early students of 22-year CBOE veteran turned teacher Dan Sheridan, regarded as one of the foremost option mentors.

When he's not trading, Greensboro, NC–based Ladd volunteers for the Service Core of Retired Executives (SCORE) organization and also at a local retirement community. He agreed to answer some questions on August 22, 2008. The interview was conducted by STOCKS & COMMODITIES contributor John Sarkett.

Managing trades once they are on is the heart and soul of option trading, and that only comes with experience.

Bill, when and how did you begin trading?

I was interested in options for several years before I began trading. After I left the pharmaceutical industry and began my own consulting business, I started to trade covered calls on stocks I currently owned, but only had limited success.

How did you come in contact with Dan Sheridan and his option mentoring service?

I met Sheridan through OptionVue. I was using OptionVue software and their representative told me about his mentoring program. So I was introduced to his style of monthly income strategy trading that way.

Some of Sheridan's students seem to specialize in condors. Is that what you do?

No, but I do trade high- and low-probability iron condors, calendars, and broken-wing butterflies. Each strategy has its own entry and exit rules. Managing trades once they are on is the heart and soul of option trading, and that only comes with experience.

What position size do you typically trade? Do you adjust the trade size month to month based on results?

I use a set dollar amount per trade each month to determine the number of contracts for a given trade. If the market is more volatile, I scale into the trades. In addition, if there is extreme volatility in the market, I reduce the allocation per trade amount, and in some cases, I just stay out of the market until it settles down.

What is your entry methodology?

It depends on the strategy. Each strategy has its own entry methodology and risk management rules. For example, a high-probability iron condor has different entry methodology than a low-probability iron condor, and they each have different risk management rules. Calendars have their own entry and exit methodology.

Where did you learn adjustments?

When I first started trading, I would just get out of a trade or roll the trade up or down. I learned from Sheridan how to effectively adjust and manage trades, and that being able to manage trades is the key to being a profitable trader. There

ABOUT CONDORS

An iron condor is a four-legged credit spread, most easily conceptualized as a put credit spread below the market and a call credit spread above the market. A high-probability condor has a "high probability" of the underlying *not* hitting the short strikes. Typically, strikes with deltas of seven or so are sold, with the next strike further out — that is, the wings — bought as protection. This might equate to something like RUT (Russell 2000 index) at 700, 600/610/800/810, that is, buy the 600 put, sell the 610 put, sell the 800 call, buy the 810 call.

The low-probability condor is sold closer to the underlying at 12–15 deltas. This might be something like 620/630/780/790 condor. It generates a higher credit, but with it, greater likelihood of an adjustment. But that's not necessarily bad; for Dan Sheridan's top students, like Ladd, "adjusting," whether rolling up, rolling down, adding debit spreads, or additional calls and puts to the underlying condor, is almost as natural as breathing. (See the sidebar, "Option adjustment," for more on the method Sheridan teaches to trade these two kinds of condors.)

—*John Sarkett*

INTERVIEW

are maybe four or five different things you can do to adjust a trade, including adding a calendar at the at-the-money (ATM) strike to buy time, scaling out, or buying extra longs to cut the delta.

What is your exit methodology?

It depends on the type of trade. Just as with the entry methodology, each strategy has its own risk management rules.

What was your motivation to sign on?

I understood the mechanics of how options worked from reading books on option trading and doing some trading on my own. After discussing the mentoring program with Sheridan, however, I realized I did not know how to trade and it was apparent that was what he could teach me. I don't think most people realize there is a *big* difference between understanding the mechanics of options and being able to trade successfully year after year.

What has been your track record? Pre-Dan, post-Dan.

Prior to working with Sheridan, I only had limited success, mostly on covered calls. In 2007, I had 10 winning months and two losing months, ending the year very successfully. But my sole income for the past three years has come from trading options.

If a trader with the capacity to follow rules undertook condor trading, what kind of annual return could he or she expect?

You do have to be disciplined, but it's more than following the rules. You have to have the personality for trading.

What's that?

Part of it is patience. Some traders start out, put on condors for a few months, then the market moves sideways and the traders beat themselves up that they didn't trade bigger. But they haven't been through all the different kinds of scenarios the market can throw at you. That's why it's so important to trade small, for six, 12, even 18 months.

Not only that, trading is like any other business or profession — some people will be better at it than others. Generally, I look at the yield per trade. On condors, I'm looking for yields of 10–13% per trade. Calendars will have a better yield than condors. With calendars, I'm looking for something in the 15% per trade range.

Here's how I figure yield:

(Margin - credit received)/gain = yield

For example, if your trade is a 20-point wide RUT 30 lot iron condor for $3.27 - margin = $60,000 - credit received = $9,810, so that's $60,000 - 9,810 = $50,190. That's the yield base. If you made $7,000 on this trade, your yield would be $7,000/$50,190 = 13.94%.

Another way to look at this trade is $7,000 out of a possible $9,810, so that's approximately 71% of the maximum amount you could have received on this trade. This is all I want out of a trade. I never carry a trade into expiration week — the delta and gamma risk are way too high for me.

What size do you trade?

In a given month, I might have on positions on the Russell 2000 index (RUT), iShare Russell 200 index (IWM), Diamond (DIA), NASDAQ 100 exchange traded fund (QQQ), S&P 500 Depositary Receipts (SPY), and maybe 20 to 30 contracts or so in each — so that's an average of 100 to 150 contracts at a time.

So that would be 10-point strikes in RUT?

No, 20. It generates a little bigger credit, but at the cost of higher margin, and a higher theoretical risk, too. Everything in trading is a tradeoff.

Which broker do you use?

Thinkorswim. They have an excellent platform, excellent customer service, and a willingness to help.

Any final comments?

You can't overemphasize the importance of a good mentor. Dan Sheridan teaches how to trade — to learn the craft, as he would say. The real strengths of his program are his emphasis on risk management and his desire that each student become a successful trader. Trading options for a living is hard work, but it's nice to know you have someone to call if you have a question.

Dan Sheridan's website and community came after my time with him, but even as one of Sheridan's early students, I still have access to the website and all its features. Trading can be a lonely business, and having someone to talk to and share ideas and thoughts with is a great help. This is what the Sheridan community provides.

Thanks, Bill.

John Sarkett is the developer of Option Wizard Scan and Scan Wizard software (http://option-wizard.com) and the author of Extraordinary Comebacks.

RELATED READING

Sarkett, John A. [2007]. "Calendar Spreads With Dan Sheridan," *Technical Analysis of* STOCKS & COMMODITIES, Volume 25: May.

_____ [2007]. "Double Calendars And Condors," *Technical Analysis of* STOCKS & COMMODITIES, Volume 25: June.

_____ [2007]. "Double Diagonals And Butterfly Spreads," *Technical Analysis of* STOCKS & COMMODITIES, Volume 25: July.

OPTION ADJUSTMENT

Option adjustment is a huge subject unto itself. Each strategy generates trading rules of its own in the Sheridan methodology. Here's how he handles one of the most common — the calendar spread, when the underlying moves against the strategist.

1. Add a calendar. After putting on a calendar spread, you would be pleased if it sat there and did nothing until expiration. Unfortunately, stocks don't do this, and it takes a bit of skill to earn your profit. So when you reach the next strike, up or down, you can consider adding another calendar. This will bring you back to breakeven or even allow you to squeeze out a small profit.

2. Partial repositioning. When the underlying has moved sufficiently for you to reach breakeven on the risk curve, you can reposition. On the move up, your delta has gone from zero, say, to -30. Say you have 10 50 calendars; take five off at 50 and put five back on at 52.50. You have likely cut your deltas now in half, to -15. If the stock starts moving sideways again, this will bring you back to breakeven, or even allow you to squeeze out a small profit. Forecast recap: slightly bullish, split decision between two strikes, 50 and 52.50.

3. Full repositioning. Say you are more bullish than that. The stock has moved up for a reason, and you agree it's worth more. Say again you have 10 50 calendars. Take all 10 off at 50 and put 10 back on at 52.50. Your -30 delta is now back to zero or thereabouts. Again, if the stock starts moving sideways again, this will create a profit opportunity. Forecast: more bullish, you have changed your opinion that the stock is now worth 52.50, not 50.

4. Roll up. Let's say you become straight-out bullish. Take in your short option and roll it up — that is, sell the next strike in the direction of the move. If you are calendar-spread at 50 and the stock increases, buy in your short 50 and sell the 52.50 strike. Keep the 50 strike call. You are now long deltas, in our example here, moving from -30 delta to +15 or +30 delta. You are now diagonally spread — that is, you have gone from a calendar spread, same strike (50), to a diagonal spread (long 50, short 52.50). You did this because your forecast is now bullish. (By this time, you have changed from a delta-neutral strategy, no movement, to a directional strategy, with a different risk-reward ratio and a different risk curve as well.)

5. Roll down. Say you become straight-out bearish — take in your short option and roll it down — that is, sell the next strike in the direction of the move. If you are calendar-spread at 50 and the stock decreases, buy in your short 50, and sell the 47.50 or 45 strike. Keep the 50 strike call. You are now short deltas, probably moving from -30 delta to -50 delta or so. You are also now diagonally spread — you have gone from a calendar spread, same strike (50), to a diagonal spread (long 50, short 47.50 or 45). You did this because your forecast is now bearish. (By this time, you have changed from a delta-neutral strategy — that is, no movement, to a directional strategy, with a different risk-reward ratio and a different risk curve as well.)

6. Closeout. If there is a material change in the situation of the underlying and you are truly confused, close the trade. Even a large move against you by this time will likely create only a small loss. Worst case: your initial debit — that is, if you put on a calendar spread for $0.40, that's the most you can lose.

7. When to take profit. Target a 20% yield. When that level is reached, take off the calendar when profit slips back a bit — that is, when it declines to 17%. At that point, either take the entire position off or roll the front month to the next. Go by the yield, don't hang around to see what the market gives you. That's the professional way to trade: *yield.*

If a calendar costs you $2,000, and you are up $400 in two weeks, protect your profit now above all else. Watch your profit like a hawk now that you have one — not deltas, thetas, stock price, or anything else. *You are protecting your profit.* If trade profit on a $2,000 calendar — once $400 — now declines to $340, exit, take your gain, thank the trading gods, move on, redeploy funds. That's it.

S&C

600 Students Later: What Dan Sheridan Has Learned as an Options Mentor

May 2009
By John A. Sarkett

For 22 years, Dan Sheridan was part of Mercury Trading, one of the top specialist firms at the Chicago Board Options Exchange. Jon Najarian (now of CNBC and OptionMonster.com) was the founder of Mercury, and his brother, Pete Najarian, joined the firm later after a long career in the NFL. Of his experience there, Sheridan says, "We were successful because we worked well as a team, and we focused on defense—the risk-management part of the business."

As market making became more a game of capital and computers versus humans, and as many firms and their principals migrated elsewhere, Sheridan also decided to leave the pits and start his own options mentoring business five years ago. He says he had a burden to teach retail traders to fish for themselves as a business. Daunting? "Yes, but I believed it could be done if retail traders employed the same tenets we used in the pits, and now we are doing it."

5 SHERIDAN TENETS

After observing and working with retail and institutional customers and mentoring them through live trades for some time, Sheridan has compiled five main tenets that all options traders should know.

1. Have Realistic Expectations: "If you suffer from insomnia or just stay up late from time to time, you've seen the late-night trading commercials that promise quick riches, lavish lifestyles and tons of free time. They even offer money-back guarantees and talk about monthly cash flow like it's an annuity. I wish!" he says. "With these unrealistic expectations, retail traders usually get discouraged quite easily because they can't understand why they are not coining money after three months. In the pit, we had a statement: If a trader can break even after six months, that's great! That's what we aim for, and from there, we go on to profitability."

2. Learn Your Craft: Sheridan shares, "If you are a doctor, pilot, CEO, carpenter or Indian chief, you didn't learn your business in a two-day seminar. I tell students they have no idea what they don't know when they start. You can't even think of running a business till you get good at the craft. Once new students are ready for live trading, I expect them to put on three to five live trades per month for six to nine months with very small trades. This foundation is essential."

Sheridan's best students have the patience to start small, stay small and gradually work up to size.

3. Plan Your Trade: "Before I get them, most retail traders basically trade by the seat of their pants," he says. "This is clearly amateur. At Mercury Trading, we had a daily morning meeting where we planned our strategy for that day. We prepared for war in a time of peace. Every trade has three components: profit target, maximum loss and adjustment point. We knew them cold. Ask yourself as a retail trader, do you do this? The answer is likely no. This planning protects us from our greatest enemy in trading: ourselves. Without a plan, we trade by our emotions and our stomach. I don't know about you, but my belly is a horrible trader."

4. Develop Market Stamina: "Why do most retail traders fail long term? The only thing that can prevent you from being a successful retail options trader is losing too much money or losing your confidence," Sheridan explains. "The biggest way to prevent this is to trade very small your first nine to 12 months. Get plenty of trades under your belt and prove to yourself you are making progress. What I do with students is something like this: I generally stress positive theta trades

for monthly income. These strategies would include calendars, credit spreads, condors, diagonals and butterflies."

Here is a sample schedule from which Sheridan has students work:

• Months 1 to 6: Use $7,000 to $10,000 in capital to engage in four to seven live trades. "The goal is simply to break even," he says, "and only move to the next level if you can at least break even on your trades for six consecutive months."

• Months 7 to 12: Use $20,000 in capital to enter four to seven live trades. Sheridan: "We raise the bar just a bit. The goal is to achieve an average of 2 percent to 3 percent per month for six months. Stay at this level until you achieve the profit targets."

• Months 13 to 18: Use $30,000 in capital to engage in four to seven live trades. "The goal now is to achieve 3 percent to 4 percent per month for six months before you increase your size," he says.

• Months 19 to 24: Use $40,000 to $50,000 in capital to engage in four to seven live trades with the goal of achieving 5 percent to 7 percent per month before increasing size.

Think about this, Sheridan says, "If your nephew Tony wanted $100,000 to $200,000 to trade options, what would you say to him? You might consider giving him $5,000 to $7,000 and see how he did. If he did well and proved he could do it, you would slowly give him some more. You would want at least two to three years of successful trading under his belt before you would part with your money.

"If that sounds condescending, it's not meant to be. At Mercury Trading it took an average of two years for a new trader to get enough experience to take the helm of the specialist ship. You have to take the time; you don't learn this stuff from books. We want our students around in two to three years. If they make money the first few months, it's from the kindness of the market, not their abilities. It takes time! Be patient.

"The good news: It can be done. We have scores of students from all walks of life all around the world who are generating excellent returns (5 percent to 7 percent per month), month in and month out."

5. Adapt to the Times: How did the market meltdown of 2008 affect Sheridan's teaching and students? As the Volatility Index (VIX) rose to historic levels last September and October, he wisely advised students to stay out of the market entirely. In November, he suggested getting back in but with extremely small amounts of capital and very slowly.

He wrote this note to students before a trip to give a seminar: "As I get ready to fly to San Francisco in the next few hours, I am thinking about the market. VIX is right at 65, the upper end of our comfort range for nondirectional monthly income trades. RVX [Russell 2000 Volatility Index] is 69.66, right at our upper number in RVX and RUT [Russell 2000 Index]. We have talked about small income trades to get our feet wet after a five-week hiatus because of the high volatility in the market.

"I want to stress *small* and just dabble. I don't know what's going to happen in the market, but if we break 450 in RUT today or tomorrow, I think we could start motoring toward 75 in the RVX, and I would probably retreat back to the sidelines. Be very comfortable with the risk/reward of your spreads.

"We want to play, that's how we learn, but we want to be wise. Speculative trades or long-term trades are a different matter, and this note is mainly addressing nondirectional income trades."

BUT DOES IT REALLY WORK?

All this stuff sounds great on paper. But in trading, there is really only one question: Does it work—in live markets, in real time, not just on paper or in the never-never land of backtesting? So what do the people on the receiving end, the actual firing line—that is, Sheridan's students—say?

As stated previously, Sheridan's students come from every walk of life, but he seems to attract a disproportionate share of former CEOs, surgeons, doctors and pilots. Some adhere to his rules absolutely—everything by the numbers. Others, interpret Sheridan's rules as principles and adapt them as they see fit.

With Sheridan's permission, I sent surveys to roughly 200 of his students by e-mail, and a high percentage replied (approximately 25 percent). Of these, each commented favorably—a statistical improbability. Sheridan must be doing something correct, I would say, in his own understated way. Students, whether successful or still learning, praise Sheridan's abilities as a mentor and his training program. (Traders quoted here requested anonymity; comments can be verified by requesting more information from Sheridan at dan@sheridanmentoring.com.)

Charles D., a trader from Atlanta wrote, "I have been trading options for over 10 years and had very mixed results. I have been following Dan's methods and have discovered what mistakes I was making and how to correct them. Since then, I have seen a 5 percent monthly gain, on average, on my trading capital using his methods. Dan has taught me that trading is a craft, and that I need to create a trading plan. ... I highly recommend his training to anyone who is tired of losing money in the markets."

Not all traders are as successful as Charles. Some still in the beginning stages are having a difficult time making profitable trades. This illustrates Sheridan's important tenet of starting out small until a trader progresses and gains confidence. Robert L. from Dalton, Ga., e-mailed, "I started with Dan in June and began live trading in September. I started with a small $7,200 account. So far, I'm in the hole, down to around $5,200, but in the last month, I've been getting more consistent in making a profit on individual trades. I consider the loss so far as just a part of the learning curve and am going to stay small until I get up to around $10,000. This may well take another six months to a year, but that is OK by me. ... I won't start trading more until I'm confident I can be successful with a little. The best thing now is that I'm trading consistently."

Another trader, from Naples, Fla., has become so proficient with Sheridan's trading method that he is achieving a year-to-date gain of more than 60 percent. Edward R. wrote, "I have been involved in options trading for five years. My primary goal when I began was to generate monthly income. During that time, I attended numerous educational seminars and heard Dan speak on several occasions. His philosophy and approach to trading was exactly what I needed. I realized it would take considerable time and effort to become skilled in his techniques. I also realized doing it on my own would be very difficult. As soon as my personal circumstances permitted, I contacted him to begin the mentoring program.

"Thanks to Dan, I have learned to develop a successful trading plan and stick with it! Entries, exits, money management are all part of it. More important, what *not* to do has proven invaluable. It is much better to avoid a bad trade than to try and fix it.

"Dan's enthusiasm and knowledge of options trading makes it easy for a student to stay focused and learn this complicated subject. His mastery of the Greeks is phenomenal, and his ability to explain potential trades and existing positions in terms of the Greeks is a skill I could have never learned on my own."

Six months after sending the survey, I went back to Edward R. to see how he was doing. He reports a year-to-date gain of 61 percent. His comment was: "Luck was with me in February and July, and I had closed out my positions before disaster occurred. But it was the way Dan taught me how to analyze my position and where to place the contingent orders that saved me in September." He added that newer, simplified teaching on adjustments greatly added to his success.

Many more plaudits racked up (see some in "A Standing Ovation"), but you get the picture.

No one cited any magic bullets being cast in the Sheridan options mentoring foundry, just the legacy of a pit mentality of sound planning, good craftsmanship, market stamina and rigid and predetermined risk management. Adrenaline, thrills and chills—not here. Some would call it boring, but since most have experienced the alternative, Sheridan's students would opt for the less "stimulating," more profitable plan.

John A. Sarkett is the author of Extraordinary Comebacks: 201 Inspiring Stories of Courage, Triumph, and Success. He created Option Wizard® software (http://Option-Wizard.com) and writes frequently on the financial markets. Dan Sheridan (dan@sheridanmentoring.com) mentors students daily from around the world via SheridanMentoring.com. His students form an active options trading community there as well, sharing trade candidates, software creations and industry news.

A STANDING OVATION

Students from all over the world have applauded Dan Sheridan's mentoring abilities and trading strategies. Here are a few more.

Tom N. from Germany, wrote, "Anyone can learn with someone experienced helping them, but Dan's patience really shines. ... He really does care about each student and wants them to succeed and be doing option trading 20 years from now!" (Author's note: Sheridan often says that when you join his group, it's for life.)

A brokerage industry professional, Fabrizio E., from London, England, wrote, "In my personal opinion (I am a director in a futures brokerage), he's a great trader, with the ability to easily transmit his knowledge—not an easy task!"

I checked back with Fabrizio some six months after the initial contact. Though unhappy with London weather, he is thrilled with his options trading. He reports a 3 percent per month gain, on average, trading index strategies. Even during his worst month, he was down only 2 percent.

Brian J., a trader from Greenville, S.C., says, "I have been trading options since spring 2006. ... My condor position ran into trouble in May 2006. ... At that time, I realized that I needed further education. ... Dan's tutelage has taught me more about options trading in a risk-controlled manner than any other source. I have a different focus after taking Dan's course."

SFO Magazine Article from:

http://www.sfomag.com/Trading_Options_News-600_Students_Later___What_Dan_Sheridan_Has_Learned_as_an_Options_Mentor-ar1345i97.aspx

Print | Close

Starting Small, Soaring Skyward

Sizing Up For Success

Here's a look at how an option trader started small and graduated to trading "more size."

by John A. Sarkett

True to his name, option trader Tony Sizemore trades "more size" than most. After a long career in mortgage lending, which included more than a passing interest in the financial markets, he turned his attention full time to options, specifically monthly income strategies from options. "This was the first time I had enough liquid capital to pursue trading as a business, and I reasoned that if I got serious about it, I could be successful as a trader," he said.

Getting the right teacher makes all the difference, and that's where things took off for Sizemore. After trading fu-

tures on his own for years with up and down results, he connected with option mentor Dan Sheridan. By employing the former CBOE trader's unique risk management methodologies, Sizemore became consistently profitable.

Gradually, Sizemore sized up, now trading a prodigious 500 to 1,000 contracts per week — and profitably (ranging annually from 41% to 119% increases), because he learned his craft and methodology slowly but surely, eventually becoming expert enough to advance and adapt as the market changed.

CBOE WEBSITE AS THE SOURCE

The strategies Sheridan was employing were similar to what Sizemore had done in the past but Sheridan's worked better because his strategies had a plan, and he showed how to adjust these strategies based on market conditions. "I began making money using the basic strategies I learned,"

JOHN NEBRASKA

OPTIONS

Sizemore says.

Although Sizemore had traded options for about 10 years, he signed up for mentoring with Sheridan. Under Sheridan's tutelage, Sizemore began trading the condor, calendar, and double diagonal. He learned that every strategy has its own place and should be managed differently, he said, adding that "knowing which type of strategy is conducive to certain market conditions."

His contract size increased over the years, and now it's not uncommon for Sizemore to trade 75 to 100 spreads on each side of a condor in the NDX, his main underlying vehicle, with 50- to 75-point strikes. On a busy week he may trade 500 to 1,000 contracts on positions that require adjustments. He also trades the SPX, XAU, US Treasury bond options, gold futures options, Dow futures options, some of the SPDRs, and individual stocks.

ENTERING THE MARKET

After his first year in the Sheridan program, Sizemore's style began to emerge. Sizemore follows Sheridan principles, but adds his own style. For condors and diagonals, he starts the week of expiration of the front month. So about the middle of expiration week, he will start positions for the next expiration month. This equates to about 25 to 35 days from expiration. For calendars and butterflies, he starts around 30 days from expiration of the front month.

Sizemore usually starts his trades with about half his intended position size, then works up as the market gyrates, looking to add to the position on some of the larger percentage days. The current implied volatility plays an important role in his strategy selection. When volatilities are high, he will look at strategies that profit from a decline in volatilities, like condors. When volatilities are low, he looks for strategies that do well when volatilities increase, such as calendars and double diagonals.

Then things get more complex. It's important to note that most strategies have different styles that can be applied such as low-probability and high-probability condors; single, double, and "campaign" calendars; "iron" and "broken wing" butterflies and so on, and these variations can be applied based on current implied volatility or market direction.

Most of Sizemore's strategies are what he refers to as freestyle. He may have a base condor, with an embedded calendar or two and a diagonal all at once as one total position. He then manages his positions based on the greeks and doesn't concern himself with adjusting based on the deltas of his short options or distance between current underlying price and breakeven points.

ADJUSTING BY THE GREEKS

For condor positions, Sizemore will adjust the position when his delta to theta ratio approaches 10%. For example, with a position theta at 4500, if his delta approaches +360 or -360 (8%), then he will look for ways to bring the delta back to a range of + or -225 (5%). He likes to keep condor deltas at or below 5% of position theta. The adjustment he makes to do

this will depend upon his outlook for implied volatility, margin considerations, and days to expiration of the front month.

Sizemore will use additional long puts as insurance on condors or other strategies as well. For put insurance he likes to use either a partial calendar or diagonal (which he refers to as a "shotgun wedding") or he'll buy a close-to-the-money put ("mouse ear"). These help him adjust his vega to where he wants it. His least favorite types of insurance are additional long positions on a credit spread, because they only help early in the trade and their benefit diminishes quickly over time. His insurance is not limited, however, to puts. Sometimes, he will use call insurance as well.

OTHER OPTION STRATEGIES

Condors are Sizemore's mainstay, but he also trades butterflies and calendars, more of the latter and usually at-the-money rather than out-of-the money looking for direction. Using some of the chief tenets of the Sheridan method, Sizemore will:

■ Put on a calendar only if the implied volatility of the options is in the lowest third of the most recent three- to six-month range. Why? A volatility crush will hurt the position as the long option will lose more than the short option. In other words, lost vega will gain theta.

■ Adjust a calendar if the underlying approaches the expiration breakeven line. The adjustment will add another calendar if the direction is down or selling a put credit spread if the direction of the underlying is up. Once the profit approaches 30% of its maximum profit at expiration, he will close it entirely or convert it to a condor position. The point is not to hold on to expiration in hopes of hitting a home run, but to harvest a reasonable profit.

To alleviate the stress of trading for a living, Sizemore likes to employ colorful names for positions or situations, such as "navigating the sea of death" (Figure 1), "time traveler" (Figure 2), and "shotgun wedding" (Figure 3).

TIME AND CHANGE

With the recent volatile markets, it's important to point out that Sizemore keeps his position guidelines fluid. This is one of the most difficult aspects of not just being profitable long term, but exceling. His adjustment methods have changed to apply to the changing environment.

In a low-volatility environment, you could take your time on adjustments, but now you have to disengage your emotions as best you can and be prepared for the market to move further than you think, up or down. Adjusting your trading instruments and guidelines periodically is not easy to do and is one of the reasons profitable option trading is difficult.

Many traders want to focus on a rigid plan based on backtesting strategies to determine the optimal rules and then trade based on the rules developed without modifying further. Back-

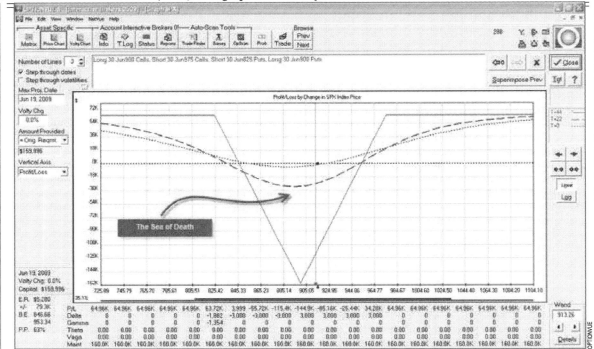

FIGURE 1: NAVIGATING THE SEA OF DEATH. The sea of death is the void in your position that must be traversed before you enter your profit zone. Some positions that require you navigate the sea of death include a ratio backspread, a long straddle, a short butterfly, and a reverse (short) calendar. Each position requires a certain navigation.

testing has many benefits, but Sizemore feels that if the trading plan has too many if/then provisions, it means you have done an excellent job of modeling the past — but to trade the future, you must remain flexible. In addition, if you make a mistake it's best to correct it, absorb the loss, and don't try to change your guidelines to accommodate the error.

CALCULATING PERFORMANCE

What has been Sizemore's actual performance? His total returns for the past few years:

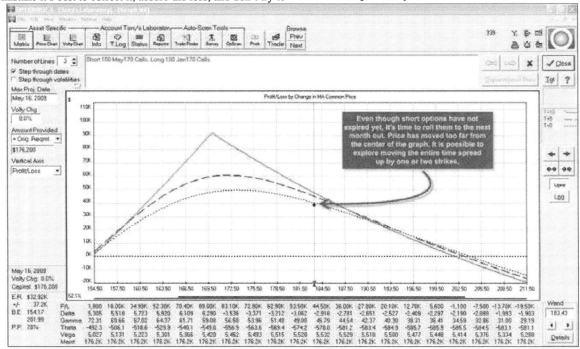

FIGURE 2: TIME TRAVELER. This is also called a campaign calendar spread. It is a calendar spread where you sell the front month and buy the expiration month several months out and continually roll your short to the next month as they expire.

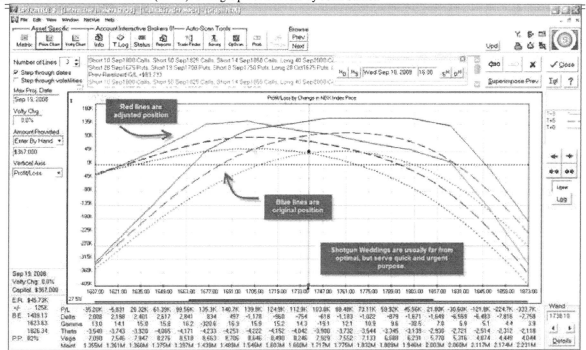

FIGURE 3: SHOTGUN WEDDING. This is an adjustment that involves "marrying," or buying, a back-month option at the same strike as a front-month short option that is under attack by the market. This is done as a quick fix and is usually not something you cherish and is temporary.

- **2006:** 64.9%
- **2007:** 119%
- **2008:** 41%. "My total return through the end of August was 67.3%," Sizemore says. "Then I lost 16% in September and another 22.2% in October. I then generated gains of 7.2% in November and 4.7% in December for a total return of 41% for 2008."

For year to date 2009, through April 15, Sizemore's return was 20.1%.

REPLICABLE?

Can anyone replicate Sizemore's success? He believes that successful option trading skills can be taught to anyone willing to put in the time required to learn. He believes that what you are taught, and how, are keys to success. Another key is to master your own emotions. "Both are a journey, not an end, with marvelous places to visit along the way," concludes Sizemore.

John A. Sarkett is the creator of Option Wizard software (http://option-wizard.com) and author of Extraordinary Comebacks: 201 Inspiring Stories Of Courage, Triumph, And Success *and a new volume 2 (see http://sarkett.com). He writes frequently on financial markets.*

SUGGESTED READING

Sarkett, John [2009]. *Extraordinary Comebacks 2*, CreateSpace.

_____ [2007]. *Extraordinary Comebacks*, Sourcebooks.

_____ [2009]. "Adjusting Option Trades With Bill Ladd," interview, *Technical Analysis of* STOCKS & COMMODITIES, Volume 27: Bonus Issue.

S&C

AT THE CLOSE

Triple Theta, Half The Time

Here's a turbocharged option strategy.

Francisco Antonio Urrutia, a former banker with a penchant for a single index option and risk management, has been generating stupendous returns for the past three years. In this niche of option exotica — several thousand individuals exclusively trading the Russell 2000 (RUT) condor — where 100 condors per month is deemed large and carries a $100,000 theoretical risk, he does five or 10 times that size on a monthly basis, and profitably. Spread across 10 different accounts, he has averaged 10% to 15% monthly returns against reg-T margins in fewer than four years. How did he get interested in the rare topic?

TURNING POINTS

"We were living in Celebration [FL], exploring market opportunities, [and] I happened to see an ad on television about an option mentoring seminar," Urrutia explained. He met Dan Sheridan, founder of Sheridan Options Mentoring

by John A. Sarkett

LISA HANEY

AT THE CLOSE

(SOM). After nearly 25 years as a Mercury Trading market maker specialist in the CBOE pits, Sheridan founded his company in 2007. Now, SOM serves an average of 150 students daily via webinar.

Urrutia said that he and his wife started the mentoring program with Sheridan, studying income strategies. They stuck with Sheridan's rules and followed his advice to stay with one-contract trades. The "rules" include stringent risk management, including predetermined entry points, predetermined max loss, predetermined adjustment points — and nothing by the seat of the pants.

After paper-trading in 2006, Urrutia scaled up, again per the Sheridan method. He moved from paper-trading to trading one contract, and then, after time, 10 contracts. At the end of 2006 he moved to 20s. He stayed with 20s for the first six months of 2007, then moved to 50s. In the third year, he moved up to 100s, eventually to his current 500-contract size. How did he fare in the terrifying markets of 2008? "I was forced to better apply the golden rules, and then I profited more," he said, adding that when the Dow Jones Industrial Average swings big in a day, there are more profit opportunities, not fewer.

INNOVATION

By this time, Urrutia was able to amalgamate the different strategies he learned into one powerful vehicle: the Russell 2000 index (RUT). Simply, on a condor base, he usually, but not always, layers a butterfly and a calendar. (More on this later.)

When the market makes big moves, especially down, everything comes down, Urrutia says. "So if everything was correlated anyway, for me it was easier to trade only one index instead of having positions in different indexes as diversification. I consider the different strategies within the R   ors, both high and lo   Russell 2000. We m

"We trade 500 contracts in the front month and 500 contracts in the next for condors under normal conditions. We put on a high-probability condor, selling deltas from seven to 10, at 50 days to expiration, and also put on low-probability condors at about 30 days, as the expiration month becomes the front month."

According to Sheridan's definition, a low-probability condor starts with deltas on the short strikes at 14–18, and a typical life span of 30 days, plus or minus. A high-probability condor starts with deltas at 10 or less and a life span of some 50 days. The "high" and "low" monikers serve only to separate the two condor types, Urrutia adds.

"We also place a 20% to 30% ratio in butterflies and calendars, at the money, half and half, depending on the volatility — for example, if he has 100 condors, he might also have 20 to 30 total of butterflies and calendars. The RUT butterflies are set 50 points wide on each side — for example, 550/600/650 on the RUT. The lower the volatility of the RUT,

the higher the ratio. When markets are wild, we scale back: we trade one third of this position when conditions are high risk.

"We enter the trades as whole positions: condors, calendars or butterflies," Urrutia concludes. "Nothing fancy. We aim to collect $2.50 to $3.50 for low-probability 14–18 short strike delta condors vs. $1.00 to $1.25 credit for a high-probability 10 delta or less short strike condor."

TIMING

"In my experience you can get in more trouble trying to time the market," Urrutia remarks. Taught to be a creature of habit to harness the probabilities, he enters his condor positions 50 or 30 days out, for "high prob" and "low prob," respectively. He is in the market every month. But before doing so, he does his homework and makes some crucial considerations.

TECHNICAL ANALYSIS

Urrutia looks for support and resistance, using simple trendlines, moving averages plus Fibonacci retracements — and a sense in "knowing" the RUT from watching it and only it all day, every day. If the RUT is butting up against resistance, he will be somewhat short deltas. Conversely, if the RUT is at support, he will be long deltas. (This may happen only a few times each year, Urrutia adds.)

What if the RUT is smack in the middle? A balanced sale results, and a delta-neutral position.

ORDER ENTRY

Unlike many condor traders, Urrutia enters the four-legs as one order. "I am willing to give $0.10 to $0.15 from the midpoints to do this, managing the position rather than trying to squeeze out a few more cents on the entry," he says. "The money is made in the risk management."

CREATING MORE THETA, REDUCING VEGA

At the same time his condor is executed, Urrutia will add both a butterfly and a calendar spread, at a 20% to 30% ratio — that is, 10 condors to two or three calendars and butterflies (combined). He does this to increase his theta (decay) and increase his vega (reduce his volatility risk).

Why not butterfly or calendar? The reason: the at-the-money butterfly is positive theta but negative vega. That means if volatility shoots up, the butterfly loses. The at-the-money calendar is positive theta also, but positive vega. That means if volatility shoots up, the calendar benefits. Using both, increases theta while dampening down volatility (vega) risk.

So far, so good. What about when the market moves? What about adjustment?

ADJUSTMENTS

First, Urrutia makes himself less vulnerable to adjustment than most condor traders because his intention is to be out of the trade one week from the Monday after expiration — sum total of exposure time: nine days.

This alone is a sharp difference to the 12- to 14-day

AT THE CLOSE

elapsed time in the typical low-prob condor trade favored by some, and the 30 to 49 days favored by others in the high-prob condor (selling options with 10 deltas farther, with a higher probability of those strikes not being hit). He cuts his time exposure alone by 25% to 82%!

Can this be accomplished on a regular basis? "Sometimes faster," he says. "It depends on the market, the greeks, the days of the week, but 10 days is a good target and often achieved."

Market velocity is the key as to which adjustment Urrutia makes. If the market does nothing, he does nothing, and sits and collects theta — the best of all possible worlds for the condor trader. However, if the market is moving up but in a controlled fashion, and Urrutia finds himself short deltas, he will get long deltas by:

- Selling some out-of-the-money (OTM) put credit spreads

- Buying calls *or*

- Offsetting some short call spreads

Conversely, if the market is moving down but in a controlled fashion, and Urrutia finds himself long deltas and losing money, he will get short deltas by:

- Selling some OTM call credit spreads

- Buying puts *or*

- Offsetting some short put spreads

When? If low-prob condor short strike deltas hit 30 or high-prob short strike deltas hit 20, Urrutia is adjusting, but as an experienced hand, he uses discretion to temper these rules. Does he try to be delta-neutral? No. Usually, it is sufficient to cut his deltas in half to two-thirds, expecting the ebb and flow of the market to come back his way.

If the market starts moving with strong velocity and it is early in the position, Urrutia will exit his butterfly at the breakeven points, as well as his short credit spreads. He will wait 24 to 48 hours to see if the RUT can stay within a standard deviation daily move for one to two days, and then reenter his position. If it is still moving rapidly, he waits. Better to wait than lose more, he says.

In addition, if the market goes through his resistance point on the upside, or support point on the downside, he exits that side of the trade. He again waits 24 to 48 hours, then determines if he will replace that side of the trade higher (or lower).

Surprisingly, Urrutia says most months in the past two years have required no adjustment. But his battle plan is always in place.

EXPECTED RETURNS

Target: 10% to 15% return per month, and 20% to 30% or higher with a portfolio margin account. Lofty goals that a hedge fund manager would kill for, but for Francisco Urrutia, who started small, followed the rules, and scaled up gradually, attainable.

John A. Sarkett is the creator of Option Wizard software (option-wizard.com) and author of Extraordinary Comebacks: 201 Inspiring Stories Of Courage, Triumph, and Success, *as well as the sequel (see Amazon.com or http://sarkett.com).*

S&C

JOHN NEBRASKA

She Braves The Market Winds

The Queen Of The Iron Condors

Find out what one trader did when her favorite trading vehicle was down 43 points one Monday, en route to a 25% July–October, top-to-bottom loss.

by John Sarkett

 her worldwide trading community, Amy Meissner is known as "the queen of the iron condors." Part of that is attitude. There was one recent day when the Russell 2000 (RUT), her favorite trading vehicle, was down 43 points en route to a 25% July–October, top-to-bottom loss.

"I wasn't worried," she explained. "First of all, the RUT was already oversold. Second, the catalyst for the loss was political wrangling in Washington over the debt ceiling, something that had been going on for months. And my short put options had only moved from -8 delta to -14 delta on the open, then -16 during the day, and 16 is where I adjust. It was manageable."

It's that kind of unflappability that makes Meissner well-suited to her role as an option queen.

THIRD TIME'S THE CHARM

Meissner began her trading in the 1990s. "I learned about options from an article I had read and I decided to give it a try," she explains. "It was much more expensive to trade back then, and only special brokerage firms would trade options."

She started by selling SPX credit spreads. The venture lasted several months before she gave it up. Meissner decided to give the option initiative another look in 2005, opening a $20,000 discretionary account with an online advisory firm. Their specialty: iron condors.

At the outset, it was steady as she goes. It took about half a year to boost the account to $28,000, a 40% return — stunning, especially in the aftermath of the 2000–01 tech meltdown.

Then came sudden destruction. "One Wednesday before expiration, I was nervous about holding through Friday, and said I wanted to cover," she recalls. "The traders assured me there was a high statistical probability of the options going out at zero." It was part of the firm's method to let options expire worthless. It was a good idea, until it's not.

You know what happened next. Trying to accumulate the last few pennies, with no risk management plan in place other than an aim for those options to expire worthless, Meissner lost $14,000 on a large down move in her account and was cut in half.

A short time later she received a postcard in the mail promoting a new service, something called "option mentoring." She was intrigued enough to give it a go, thinking that with some hard work she would be better able to manage her *own* funds versus trusting others with a discretionary account.

So she went back to school, this time into the school of risk management. It was her best investment, she says now, and with annual returns averaging 22.46% since trading on her own, it has repaid itself many times since then.

Classic high-probability condor trading	Meissner method
Vehicle: Russell 2000 index, the RUT	
Entry	
45 to 60 days before expiration	80 to 88 days before expiration (had started with 35 days, then 60 days, settled on longer time frame)
Deltas	
Sell 8 to 10 deltas on short strikes, both puts and calls	Sell 8 deltas on short put strikes, sell 12 deltas on short call strikes
Long strikes	
10 points beyond short strike — that is, "10 wide"	30 points beyond short strike — that is, "30 wide"
Typical credit	
$1 to $1.50 for 10 wide	$4 for 30 wide
Adjustment point	
Short delta 20 to 25	Earlier: short deltas at 16, had started at 20 delta, but considers that too late now
Max rolls	
2-3	2-3
Exit target timing	
Aims to be out week before expiration	Aims to be out approximately three weeks before expiration — for example, 80-day condor
Exit spreads	
$0.25 each (range varies widely by trader)	$0.40 each
Target gain	
75% of initial credit	70%-80% of initial credit
Typical contract size of "large-size" trader	
100	25
Expects losses	
Two months per year	Two months per year
Max loss	
100% to 150% of average monthly credit	100% to 150% of average monthly credit
Funds at risk at trade opening	
$85,000 to $90,000	$52,000 to $65,000
Target annual gain	
100%	100%

FIGURE 1: THE METHOD. Here you see the classic high-probability condor trading versus Meissner's method for trading the RUT.

Six years later, Sheridan Option Mentoring is still part of her team. It was Dan Sheridan who nicknamed her "queen of the iron condors." Meissner is "one of the most professional traders in our community, and one of the most consistent," he says. "She will tweak her approach from time to time, but by and large, she approaches the market with admirable discipline, and as a result, she reaps the rewards."

THE METHOD
Meissner's methods have been refined a bit since she started trading iron condors, but here's her latest methodology (Figure 1). Approximately 80 to 88 days out she will sell a Russell 2000 iron condor. She sells the puts at minus 8 delta or so, the calls at 12 delta or thereabouts, and then buys coverage some 30 points higher on the calls, 30 points lower on the puts. She aims to generate an approximate $4 credit against a $30 risk. The total cash credit then would be about $4,000 for every 10 contracts — that is, $4 credit x 10 contracts x $100 per contract.

Should the market move against her, which is often the case, she will adjust at -16 delta, meaning that if the market declines, she will buy in her put credit spread, and then resell it 30 RUT points lower. She will sell 150% of the original size as well to make up for the loss (if the original position was 20 contracts, she will sell 30 on the adjustment). She can do this two or three

Trying to accumulate the last few pennies, Meissner lost $14,000 on a large down move.

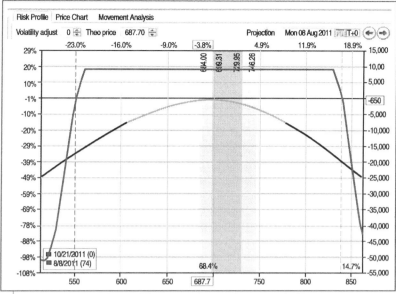

FIGURE 2: OUT OF THE STARTING GATE, DAY 1 OF A RUSSELL 2000 IRON CONDOR. In a down market, when deltas of short strikes go from -8 to -16, Meissner buys in the original short put credit spread and replaces it 30 points lower. At that time, she'll also look to take off the call credit spread and not replace it lower, unlike some traders. "No tolerance for whiplash," she says. The process is reversed, should the market move higher.

Recently, Meissner purchased an electric motor-assist bicycle, a nice metaphor for her ability to manage the winds of market change.

times before giving up on a trade and either taking a loss or scratching out.

If the market declines and the call credit spread goes to 0.40 or under (from an original $2 or so), she will exit, and *not* resell it lower. This removes the possibility of whiplash should the market bounce back up and cause a new call spread to become a loser very quickly. The process is reversed to the upside (Figure 2).

Changes over the years include days to expiration and entry style. She began with more customary 30- and 60-day condors, one of each, but she has now settled on the longer time frame due to the volatility in the market. She originally legged into the trade, selling put credit spread side when the market was down, selling the call credit spread when the market rebounded, but since then has decided it is simpler, more effective, and more carefree to put it all on at once, because losses on one side will be offset by gains on the other.

Unlike many traders whose ambition is to get big as fast as possible, which for most means 100-contract condors and up, thus theoretically putting $90,000 and more of risk on the table each month, Amy Meissner is more stealth. For every 100 contracts of a typical 10-point condor, she will trade 25 contracts of a 30-point condor instead, cutting her risk to about $65,000.

Why not 10-point wide strikes in her RUT condors, like most everyone else in options? Adjusting large quantities of contracts is a factor. Start with 25, roll twice for adjustments, and you wind up with about 55 to 60 contracts, versus 225 with a 100-contract start increased twice at 150%. Fifty-five contracts is much more manageable than 225 contracts, Meissner says.

Her profit target is approximately 80% of the original credit. If she is taking in $10,000 on a typical trade on initiation (25 contracts x $4 x $100 per point on the RUT), and she can offset her positions and capture $8,000, she's out. Often this is the case after 45 days.

THERE WILL BE BLOOD
There will be losers as well. It is part of the business, expected and managed. Meissner describes the process as "three or four steps forward and one step back." On

RUT Iron Condors 2011

Exp. month	Total adjust-ments	% Gain vs. max risk	% Gain of original credit
Jan	4	1.46	31.10
Feb	0	12.57	86.48
Mar	1	8.86	81.34
Apr	2	7.74	84.55
May	0	12.31	86.85
Jun	1	7.78	79.01
Jul	1	8.07	80.56
Aug	1	8.30	73.92
Oct	2	8.84	88.93
Nov	2	8.48	81.70
Dec	3	5.91	77.50
Totals	17	90.35	851.96
Average over 11 months traded	1.55	8.21	77.45

Did not trade Sept Exp

All calculations were made after commissions
% Gain vs. max. risk is based on the maximum T-Reg risk margin during the life of the trade (all trades done within same exp month)
% Gain of original credit is the amount of the profit realized vs. the original credit received

FIGURE 3: PERFORMANCE IN 2011. Meissner will typically expect to lose or break even one or two or even three months a year (though in 2011 there were no monthly losses) but keeps the losses to 100% to 150% of her typical monthly credit — that is, $10,000 or so.

the monthly level, she will typically expect to lose or break even one or two or even three months a year (though in 2011 there were no monthly losses, as you can see from Figure 3) but keeps the losses to 100% to 150% of her typical monthly credit — that is, $10,000 or so. Employing some quick math, if she can generate about $8,000, 10 months per year, and expect losses twice of $10,000, she can still net something like $60,000 per year, just with the RUT condor alone. And do it without breaking much of a sweat.

PIECES AND PROSPECTS

Here are a few odds and ends of Meissner's trading strategy:

■ She uses *Investors Intelligence* to help formulate a market opinion. This helps her get a handle on oversold and overbought conditions and gives her a second opinion useful for determining adjustment sizes, leaning her deltas to long and short, and so on.

■ She likes to enter condors on Thursdays or Fridays to gain weekend decay.

■ She sets alerts for both RUT and deltas, sending messages to her emails and smartphone. This helps her get off the screen as well.

■ She is part of a larger trading community via Sheridan Option Mentoring. She appropriates new ideas and concepts and also contributes as a thoughtful webinar interview subject. There are some six-plus hours of her discussions archived on the site, plus other discussions on her methods.

Boiling it down as simply as possible, Meissner earns her monthly checks by rolling her credit spreads. She aims to increase her returns going forward by being more consistent, to make her condor work an even smoother-running money machine.

Recently, she purchased an electric motor-assist bicycle to help her make her 25-mile bike expeditions a little easier against the ocean winds, a nice metaphor for her powerful ability to tame and manage the winds of market change.

John Sarkett is the creator of Option Wizard software (option-wizard.com) and author of Extraordinary Comebacks: 201 Inspiring Stories Of Courage, Triumph, and Success, *as well as the sequel (for more information, see Amazon.com or http://sarkett.com). Sarkett may be reached at jas@option-wizard.com. For more about Dan Sheridan, see http://www. sheridanmentoring.com.*

SUGGESTED READING

Sarkett, John A. [2010]. "Triple Theta, Half The Time," At The Close, *Technical Analysis of* STOCKS & COMMODITIES, Volume 28: May.
‡THJ Systems

Consistency Above All

The Calendar King

In options, consistency wins. Here's how one option trader fared using this concept.

by John A. Sarkett

A calendar spread is among the simplest of option strategies, yet among the most durable and profitable. A simplified explanation: the strategist sells a near-month contract and buys a far month against it. The near month loses value faster than the back month, and that is how a profit is generated.

As in most things, there is more to it than that, and that is why two years into the practice of trading calendar spreads, trader Himanshu Raval sought out an option mentor to learn the greeks. He found Dan Sheridan on a CBOE website video. Sheridan traded as an IBM market maker in his 24-year CBOE career, including thousands of calendars, so he knew whereof he taught.

Raval signed on as a student, and as a result, he doubled his returns from the 5% to 10% per month range to a 15% to 20% per month level, becoming something of a star in the option mentoring community.

He holds forth on the merits of a consistent approach. A meticulous recordkeeper, in the past year he has earned 18% per month on his IBM calendars with an average of 25 to 27 days in a trade.

WHY IBM?

Historically, IBM has moved less than 8% per month on average. The less the underlying moves, the better for the calendar spreader. Raval also tried other tickers — JNJ, PG,

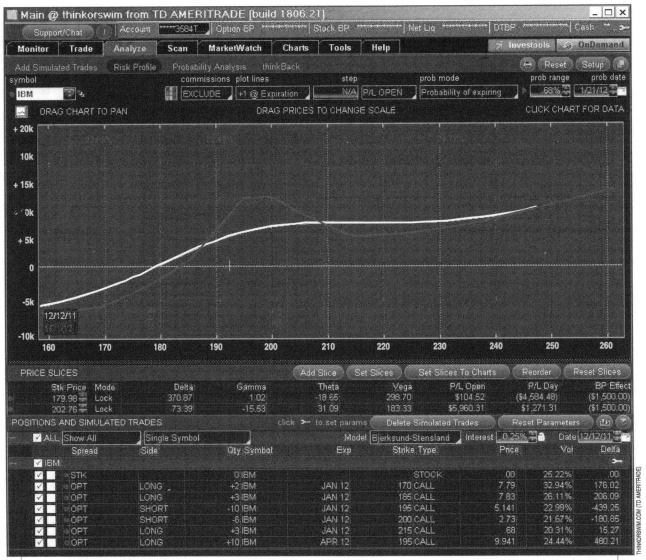

FIGURE 1: AN ELASTIC APPROACH. Risk curve of IBM triple calendar (175, 185, 190) at the end of a long, profitable ride. Raval varies number of calendars from one to three, and time of calendar spreads between four and 12 months, depending on his readings of volatility and market direction, but one thing remains constant: he is in the market each month.

and DIA — but like many professional traders before him, he settled on Big Blue, IBM. Here's how he does it.

ELASTIC APPROACH

Raval seeks to initiate a calendar position 40 to 45 days before the expiration of the short options. When volatilities are expected to either remain low or trend slowly higher, he takes bigger positions, both in size and number of strikes. A low volatility setting may find him starting with a triple calendar, with one calendar at-the-money (ATM), and then bracket that with calendars five or 10 points above and below. For example, if IBM is at 180, he may put on calendars at 180, 185, and 175.

If volatilities are high and expected to decline, the enemy of the calendar since the back month loses more than the front, and the position becomes flat or a loser, he may start with only one calendar ATM, and after that add calendars as the market moves.

Raval aims to pay the midprice (exact middle between bid and ask for the spread) but will at times pay up to 0.20 higher.

To cut his vega risk — that is, declining volatility — he also takes short vega positions via butterfly positions that bracket his calendar above (see Figure 1). He typically uses these to cut his vega risk in half. His option portfolio is divided to achieve this goal like this:

20%	IBM calendars
20%	SP calendars
20%	RUT butterflies (calls only)
20%	SPX butterflies (calls only)
20%	Cash

Small losers are part of the business, Himanshu Raval says, just not huge losses.

The butterflies are call only, not "iron" — that is, short call, short put credit spreads.

ART AND SCIENCE OF ADJUSTMENT

Himanshu Raval is a strict disciplinarian when it comes to adjustment. He adjusts when the price of the underlying reaches between the expiration breakeven and the short strike, a number he calculates in advance. He will then typically take off 50% to 100% of the position, and roll up or roll down to a new position that brackets the price of the underlying.

Here's some further risk management — when a position loses 20%, he closes it quickly without remorse. He knows from history that he can make up that amount in a month or so. Small losers are part of the business, he says, just not huge losses.

EVER THE STUDENT

Always studying and learning (he backtested calendar strategies for a total of 2,000 hours when he began his new profession), after the 2008 market crash, Raval added a technical analysis component to his trading. If IBM, his no. 1 underlying, is above its 20-day moving average, he starts his position slightly long delta. If IBM is below its 20-day moving average, he starts his position slightly short delta. "A body in motion tends to stay in motion," he says, citing the theory behind this tactic. He further explains: "In 2008, it wasn't the crash that hurt me, because higher volatilities are positive for calendar traders. It was the directional grind in the aftermath of 2008 that was compromising profits. So I took steps to lean the way the market was leaning. It has made a positive difference."

How much time between the short month and the long month? It can vary between four and 12 months, Raval says. Again, this is a function of his reading the market meteorology. If volatilities are high and possibly due for a decline, the shorter period applies. If volatilities are low, and possibly due to stay flat or increase, he will go out beyond four months, to five, six, seven, or even 12 months, the latter on a recent stock calendar trade.

What about other strategies, like iron condors? Raval has tried them. He loved the concept of "free money, great stuff, you get money for nothing" but found the roughly 9:1 risk/reward ratio of most typical condors to be extremely unfavorable (risk $9 to make $1). Instead, he found calendars to be the "most forgiving" of option strategies, and the easiest to manage. "I have yet to find someone lazier than me," he says, (which by now you can guess not to be true, but you get the idea).

Check in with him down the line, and you'll likely learn of a new tweak or two, but the mainstay — being in the market with IBM calendars every month, month in and month out — doesn't change.

Consistency is the thing. "We never teach anyone to copycat," mentor Sheridan says, "but rather learn the ropes yourself. And most important of all, be consistent, to be in the market month in and month out. That is Raval's reason for success. It's not the option strategy per se, it's not the underlying per se, it's the consistency of approach and the tweaking that comes of accurately reading of market volatility that creates success for Raval or anyone else. It's also being part of a community of traders dedicated to continuous learning and sharing. It's the process, and we're never done learning. We work on the craft every day."

Himanshu Raval has carried his desire to grow and learn even further: He is studying to become a Chartered Market Technician. He hopes to reap the rewards of his hard work for years to come.

Actually his aspirations run even further. A believer in reincarnation, he hopes to bring his financial prowess back to the next life as well, and the one after that.

John Sarkett is the creator of Option Wizard software (option-wizard.com) and author of Extraordinary Comebacks: 201 Inspiring Stories Of Courage, Triumph, And Success, *as well as the sequel (for more information, see Amazon.com or http://sarkett.com). Sarkett may be reached at jas@option-wizard.com. For more about Dan Sheridan, see http://www.sheridan-mentoring.com.*

SUGGESTED READING

Sarkett, John A. [2012]. "The Queen Of The Iron Condors," *Technical Analysis of* STOCKS & COMMODITIES, Volume 30: July.

_____ [2010]. "Triple Theta, Half The Time," *Technical Analysis of* STOCKS & COMMODITIES, Volume 28: May.

‡Thinkorswim.com

Find similar articles online at Traders.com

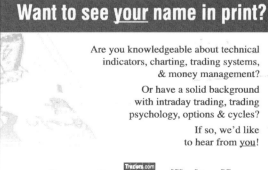

Option Wizard® Financial features John A. Sarkett

Option Wizard®

Financial Features

John A. Sarkett

for
Technical Analysis of Stocks and Commodities
SFO magazine
Futures

| OPTIONS |

Time And Options Probabilities

For traders who want to use options to hedge their long positions, here are the formulas for calculating the probabilities.

by John A. Sarkett

What's the probability that Intel [INTC] will be above 110 at a certain point? Three months from now, six months, a year? If you were to ask random-walk partisans, they would be likely to tell you, "There's no way to know." You would get the same answer from those who disparage market timers. But change the time frame to a more manageable short-term window — say, the week or two before the very next options expiration — and a little-known formula would be able to give you the exact mathematical probability.

Time is the key. Filter with technical indicators such as trend, moving average, oscillators and your own judgment, and you can use the estimated probability to your advantage by selling out-of-the-money† option premiums. Typically, the odds will favor your sale about 66% of the time, leaving just a 33% possibility that the buyer on the other side will actually call away your stock. Lending further credence to this strategy, economists at the Options Clearing Corp. report that, on average, 67% of all options expire at zero or at a loss.

If you are more conservative and don't wish to have your stock called, you can further reduce risk by buying even further out-of-the-money premium and creating a credit spread, or by simply closing your position at a loss.

While examples of selling out-of-the-money calls against stock that you own are presented here, the principles may be adapted to numerous other options strategies, including selling puts, spreads, straddles and so on. Knowing your probability of success will help put you on the right side of the trade, whatever strategy you employ.

THE EQUATION
The probability formula looks intimidating, but it can be calculated in Excel. Here is the mathematical version:

$$N\left(\frac{\left|\log\left(\frac{S_t}{K}\right) + (T-t)\left(r - \frac{\sigma^2}{2}\right)\right|}{\sigma * \sqrt{T-t}}\right)$$

where:
C = A call option
N = Cumulative normal distribution function (NORMSDIST in Excel)
t = Current time
T = Expiration date of C
K = Strike price of C
S_t = Current price of stock
r = Instantaneous rate of return of S (current risk-free interest rate)
σ = Standard deviation of returns of S

Take for example the Dell February 1997 75 calls. With the stock trading in the 66s on February 3, 1997, the 75 calls could be sold for $^1/_2$ to $^3/_4$ (55% volatility), not a princely sum, but one with the odds working for you, decay working for you, and the clock working for you — all at once.

Why the 75s? With earnings due out February 25, 1997, while 75 looked pretty distant, nevertheless, it was achievable, and in the running bull market for technology stocks, you didn't want to have your stock called away.

All this, of course, applies to the 70 and 65 calls — more premium generated, to be sure, but also a greater chance of having the stock called away. Let's work through the numbers:

C = A call option
t = Current time, February 3, 1997
T = Expiration date of C, February 21, 1997
K = Strike price of C, 75
S_t = Current price of S, 66
r = Interest rate during life of option, 0.07
σ = Standard deviation of returns of S, or implied volatility, 0.55

$$P = N\left\{\frac{\left|\log\left(\frac{S_t}{K}\right) + (T-t)\left(r - \frac{\sigma^2}{2}\right)\right|}{(\sigma * \sqrt{T-t})}\right\}$$

$$P = \text{NORMSDIST}\left\{\frac{\left|\log\left(\frac{66}{75}\right) + (0.0493)\left(0.07 - \frac{0.55^2}{2}\right)\right|}{(0.55 * \sqrt{0.0493})}\right\}$$

$$P = \text{NORMSDIST}\left(\frac{(-0.0555) + (0.0493) * (-0.0813)}{0.1221}\right)$$

$$P = 14\%$$

MIKE CRESSY

So with a 31.30% prospect of getting your stock called — or put another way, a 68.7% possibility to collect the premium while holding on to your Dell stock — let's say you sell the Dell February 75 calls for $1/2$ to $3/4$. Figure 1 is a table of the probabilities for calls and puts with the strike price at 75 on February 3, 1997.

So what actually happened in the real world?

Despite a surge in the stock price to 76 on February 19, 1997, that caused the option to surge to $1^3/_4$ (Figure 2), Dell closed at $71^1/_8$ on February 21 (Figure 3), and the 75 call expired worthless.

Here are two more examples. Looking forward, Figure 4 displays a table of probabilities on April 11, 1997, for the options with a strike of 75 and the expiration on January 16, 1998. With Dell trading at 66, there is an estimated probability of 40.34% of your stock being called by January 1998. If we shorten our time horizon to only two weeks, despite an increase in price from $66 to $71, the probability would decline to 38.26% (Figure 5).

The examples illustrate that to achieve maximum hedge effect, you may wish to cover half your position about two weeks before expiration and the other half on a price surge.

TABLE OF PROBABILITIES

		Today's in-the-money probability		
		Price ($)	Call (%)	Put (%)
Ticker symbol: DELL		$71	40.99%	59.01%
Days from now	8	70	39.05	60.95
Price increment	1	69	37.10	62.90
Stock price (minus dividends)	$66.00	68	35.15	64.85
1. Strike price	75	67	33.22	66.78
Today's date	2/3/97	66	31.30	68.70
2. Expiration	2/21/97	65	29.40	70.60
Days to expiration	18	64	27.53	72.47
Time remaining as % of a year	0.0493	63	25.70	74.30
3. Risk-free interest rate	0.0700	62	23.90	76.10
4. Implied volatility	55.00%	61	22.14	77.86
5. Dividends	$0	12/25/97	Dividend 1	
(During life of option)	$0	3/25/98	Dividend 2	
Overwrite dates and amounts	$0	6/23/98	Dividend 3	
	$0	9/21/98	Dividend 4	
Present value (PV) of future dividends	$0			
6. Stock or index price	$66			
Stock price - PV future dividends	$66			

FIGURE 1: The price column is the projected price. The call and put columns estimate the probabilities for calls and puts with the strike price at 75 on February 3, 1997. The option probability formula estimated the chances of the 75 calls being called on February 21, 1997, at 31.30%.

TABLE OF PROBABILITIES

		Today's in-the-money probability		
		Price ($)	Call (%)	Put (%)
Ticker symbol: DELL		$71	42.90%	57.10%
Days from now	1	70	42.40	57.60
Price increment	1	69	41.90	58.10
Stock price (minus dividends)	$66	68	41.38	58.62
1. Strike price	75	67	40.86	59.14
Today's date	4/11/97	66	40.34	59.66
2. Expiration	1/16/98	65	39.80	60.20
Days to expiration	280	64	39.27	60.73
Time remaining as % of a year	0.7671	63	38.72	61.28
3. Risk-free interest rate	0.0700	62	38.17	61.83
4. Implied volatility	55.00%	61	37.61	62.39
5. Dividends	$0	12/25/97	Dividend 1	
(During life of option)	$0	3/25/98	Dividend 2	
Overwrite dates and amounts	$0	6/23/98	Dividend 3	
	$0	9/21/98	Dividend 4	
Present value (PV) of future dividends	$0			
6. Stock or index price	$66			
Stock price - PV future dividends	$66			

FIGURE 4: The call and put columns estimate the probabilities for calls and puts with the strike price at 75 on April 11, 1997. The option probability formula esitmated the chances of the 75 calls being called on January 16, 1998, at 40.34%.

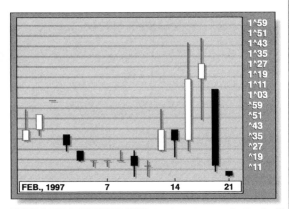

FIGURE 2: DELL FEBRUARY 75 CALLS. Despite a price surge, the 75 calls still expired at zero.

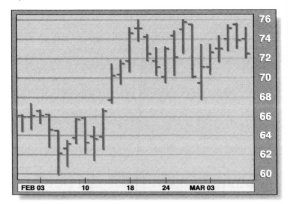

FIGURE 3: DELL. Here was the trading activity for February.

That way, if the stock were to continue sideways to down, you would collect some premium. If the stock were to surge before expiration, you would also capture some of that price movement in premium. Few things are more exasperating than to write call premium, only to have the stock surge the next day! Even if this happens, don't despair. The probabilities remain in your favor, and regression may likely ensue. Writing premium is a strategy for the patient.

And writing premium is also for the stoic. Even though you will typically have a 66% chance to collect premium and keep the stock — the market equivalent of having your cake and eating it, too — the 33% chance will invariably arise that your stock will be called away. If the stock has the meteoric possibilities of a US Robotics or Dell and it has the potential to double in the next six to 12 months, you will want to mitigate this indignity with a strategy.

OTHER STRATEGIES

If your stock turns out to have the potential to be a shooting star, you would best be served by examining your choices and coming up with a new strategy. Here are three to consider:

TABLE OF PROBABILITIES

		Today's in-the-money probability	
		Price ($)	Call (%)	Put (%)
Ticker symbol: DELL		76	52.63%	47.37%
Days from now	2	75	49.80	50.20
Price increment	1	74	46.93	53.07
Stock price (minus dividends)	$71	73	44.04	55.96
1. Strike price	75	72	41.15	58.85
Today's date	1/1/98	71	38.26	61.74
2. Expiration	1/16/98	70	35.40	64.60
Days to expiration	15	69	32.58	67.42
Time remaining as % of a year	0.0411	68	29.81	70.19
3. Risk-free interest rate	0.0700	67	27.12	72.88
4. Implied volatility	40.00%	66	24.52	75.48
5. Dividends	$0	12/25/97	Dividend 1	
(During life of option)	$0	3/25/98	Dividend 2	
Overwrite dates and amounts	$0	6/23/98	Dividend 3	
	$0	9/21/98	Dividend 4	
Present value (PV) of future dividends	$0			
6. Stock or index price	$71			
Stock price- PV future dividends	$71			

FIGURE 5: The call and put columns estimate the probabilities for calls and puts with the strike price at 75 on January 1, 1998. The option probability formula estimated the chances of the 75 calls being called on January 16, 1998, at 38.26%.

- **Buy further out-of-the-money calls.** You could have purchased the 80 calls as insurance. With the stock at 71, you would feel you wasted your dollars — but only if you also feel you waste your money on home, health and car insurance. If the stock were at 100, however, you would feel quite differently.
- **Enter buy stop.** Determine in advance where you will reenter the market. Employ your knowledge of fundamentals, technical analysis, trendlines.
- **Close your option position.** In the day or two before

expiration, most of the time premium will be gone, credited to your account, and all that will be left is the stock-option price parity. What can you do? You can buy back your call, and keep your stock to play another day.

All these steps may be viewed as the costs of doing business — a profitable business most of the time, one with costs and risks just like other businesses, but one in which you can calculate your probability of success and take appropriate action.

John A. Sarkett is active in the financial markets and is the developer of the Option Wizard put-call pricer for Excel, which includes the probability formulas described above.

RELATED READING AND RESOURCE

McMillan, Lawrence G. [1992]. *Options as a Strategic Investment*, 3d edition, Simon & Schuster/New York Institute of Finance.

Option Wizard Web site http://homepage.interaccess.com/~jas/option_ wizard.html.

†See Traders' Glossary for definition

Top 10 options mistakes

There are as many ways to lose money in the options markets as there are traders. Some mistakes, however, are repeated over and over again. Here are the 10 most common ways traders lose it all, together with some basic advice on how to avoid those mistakes.

By John A. Sarkett, developer, OptionWizard Scan software

Every now and then we hear how famous traders get blown out of the market, usually because of a mistake that with a little help of hindsight should have been easily avoided. But anybody who has placed an options or futures trade knows that whether you're a seasoned pro or a beginner, it's never too late to make that fatal mistake in the fast-paced markets. Here are 10 common examples of traders and their dooms-day mistakes. If you recognize yourself, hopefully you've corrected the problem and carried on. If you don't, be forewarned -- these seemingly simple mistakes have tripped up the best.

1 *I have a $45,000 options account, and I need to make $100,000 per year from it. I believe I can do it because I quit my job, attended seminars and will work full-time at it. Besides, I am very smart, very successful and was the youngest graduate in the history of my law school.*

This is the Unrealistic Expecter. Often successful in a previous life, he expects to be successful in options but without the requisite training or skills.

After spending a small fortune on seminars and despite warnings from others about how successful and energetic individuals may encounter problems when switching their focus to the markets, which rewards passivity, a professional quits his law practice to trade options. He springs into action on tips from his seminar gurus, trades without stops and expects the market to fork over big profits because he is on the scene and has always won. At the outset, he experiences the worst outcome possible -- he starts winning. But soon enough, the tide turns. Buying outrageous volatility, his long positions -- and he is only long -- decline until his capital expires.

This story is repeated hundreds of times each day. To avoid it, set a realistic goal, for example, 10% to 30% per year of your trading capital. If you can beat the S&P 500 consistently, you will be in the top 20% of professional fund managers.

2 *I get all my ideas from _____ (fill in the blank with your favorite guru, advisory service or broker).*

This is the True Believer in Gurus. This person prefers a black-and-white world. Shades of gray unsettle him. From time to time you may hear him ex-claim: "This has to be so -- it says so right here in black and white."

Instead of developing a well-informed opinion of the markets, it is much easier to buy a subscription to a newsletter, Web site or fax service. This approach also provides a scapegoat when things go wrong. And things do go wrong, for advisors as well as individual traders. In the fast-moving options world, this is a special danger. For instance, if you had followed *Barron's* bearish posture through the 1990s, you would have sat out or shorted the biggest bull market in history. But the solution is simple enough: Do your own work and don't rely on so-called gurus!

3 *I trade whenever the opportunity presents itself. You have to play to win, right?*

This is the Overtrader. He knows that if you try hard enough, you've got to succeed. But like a martial arts master, the market uses this otherwise positive trait against him.

A famous seminar guru counsels customers to bring a cell phone to the meeting because at the break they will call their broker and make a trade. But how do you know there is a trade to be made at 10:30 a.m. on Tuesday? How do you develop and test a system you trust in between registration and the break? Also, a lot of so called "opportunities" just aren't.

In *Reminiscences of a Stock Operator*, the legendary

speculator Jesse Livermore says he made most of his money sitting. Investment biker, CNBC host and Market Wizard Jimmy Rogers puts it this way: "I don't trade until I see a pile of money sitting in the corner. Then I go over and pick it up." And: "I don't think of myself as a trader. I think of myself as someone who waits for something to come along."

4 *I really don't need to know much about the stock -- if the option is moving, that's all I need.*

This is Mr. Twice Smart. He knows that because everyone knows about the big, successful stocks, the real answer must be in the little, unknown stocks.

Many losing traders are in small stock option positions. If the world doesn't know your stock, the world is not going to move in, buy and push it higher. Better to follow Microsoft or Intel than the software wannabes. Better to follow Lilly, Pfizer or Merck than a biotech that is perpetually on the brink of having a product approved. Microsoft, Intel and Lilly are real companies with real products and real earnings. Millions, not hundreds, follow the stocks. When the companies move, the institutions move and the stocks move.

5 *I buy the option when there is news on the stock.*

This is the News Call Buyer. He doesn't understand the volatility component of options -- he believes stock and options prices always are linked and move in lockstep. The problem is typically the next day the stock goes down and the option collapses.

This is an extremely popular approach. News services now sell pagers to alert you to financial news wherever you are. Unfortunately, buying on the news opens a Pandora's Box of trading issues: News increases volatility, which in turn increases options prices. There are two kinds of volatility. Historical volatility is a measure of how much a stock may be up or down one year from now based on past price movement. Implied volatility is the same measure but is based on the current option price. High implied volatility typically regresses to historical levels. That means after the news, the stock can stay the same or decline slightly while your option can collapse.

6 *There really is no time to follow the technicals of a stock or to bother with options analysis such as volatility, delta or in-the-money probability when you're trading options.*

For Mr. Gotta Move Fast there's no time to plan a trade. If the broker or guru speaks, he must act immediately or lose out.

Too many losing traders don't know what the technical situation in the stock was when they bought the option. But by having a clear understanding of the trend, momentum and the volume pattern, you can put the odds in your favor. You can buy a call when a stock is moving out of oversold support with a positive volume formation or, conversely, sell a call or buy a put when a stock is overextended.

Using an options calculator, it shouldn't take more than a minute to calculate volatility and delta. Implied volatility is, in effect, the option's price. You must compare implied to historical volatility to know whether your option is fairly, over- or underpriced. And don't just concentrate on what can go right, consider what can go wrong and make sure the odds are in your favor. When you trade, make it your trade with fundamental, technical and option analysis, with your target profit and your stop loss. Treat your wins and losses the same, and in time you will succeed.

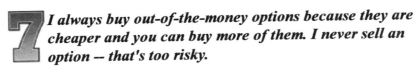 *I always buy out-of-the-money options because they are cheaper and you can buy more of them. I never sell an option -- that's too risky.*

This is the Bargain Hunter. For him, an option that loses half its value in one week is not risky because "you know how much you can lose."

Those out-of-the-money options are cheap for a reason. They have a low delta, which means that the price of the option will change very little when the price of the underlying changes. They also have a low probability of being in-the-money. One of the advantages you have as an options trader is strategy. You can employ leverage, time, expiration and limited dollar risk as friends or foes. Consider, for instance, these alternatives:

If your capital is limited, one option is an at-the-money call debit spread. (For example, for a $40 stock, buy the 40 strike, sell the 45.) Or for a put credit spread, you could sell the 40 put and buy the 35. Not only will these strategies give you a lower entry price but a higher probability of success as well. The tradeoff is that they will limit your maximum profit potential. If you own the stock, you can sell the call to collect additional income. But you also can sell the overpriced premium just before expiration with a high probability of success.

 I buy the calls when a stock splits because I know the stock has to go higher.

This is the Split Buyer. He knows that if a stock splits, it has to go higher every time.

In a raging bull market, this play has become a favorite. It also has become a somewhat self-fulfilling prophecy but less so each time because there is no fundamental reason why a pie cut into eight pieces instead of four is worth more. But when a stock splits, the calls usually become quite expensive because buyers rush in, bid them up, increase implied volatility and the call price. The next day, when volatility returns to normal, the calls decline.

If the stock is not a stalwart, consider fading the split by selling calls or buying puts. Only buy calls if you have other fundamental and technical reasons for doing so. Be sure your options are fairly priced, with a delta of 60 or more.

 I don't like to put in a stop loss or trailing protective stop. I might get stopped out. I'll just "watch it."

This is Mr. No Stops for Me Please. But he really should be called Mr. No Stops for Me Because I am Unwilling to Lose Any Money.

Carrying losses will hurt you in several ways. Not only will it deplete your financial and emotional capital, but it also will cause you to miss other big opportunities while you're wishing and hoping for your position to come back.

When you have a winner, insert a protective stop. Options are so leveraged that if your position falls back, it likely will continue much lower. Better to take half a win than to turn a winner into a loser. Otherwise, it's very hard on the psyche. Turning a winner into a loser invariably will create a "get even" mentality that will lead to further losses.

Alex Jacobsen, vice president of the Chicago Board Options Exchange puts it this way: "Like a successful gambler, you must learn to ante and fold. Ante and fold. Ante and fold. Occasionally, double up to win big."

10 *If it weren't for (insert guru, advisor, author), then I would be successful.*

This is Mr. It Wasn't My Fault. This is the one of the last comments you hear before he is forced to leave the game.

Don't blame anyone else for your trades. If you choose among great companies with expanding earnings (or the reverse for the short side), analyze the fundamentals, technicals and options (fair value, volatility, delta, probabilities), make your forecast and treat options like the business it is, you will have a greatly improved chance to succeed -- on your own, with no need to blame or credit anyone else. You will have turned options into a satisfying business enterprise instead of a bedeviling game.

John A. Sarkett is a trader and the developer of Option Wizard® Scan and author of Option Wizard Trading Method, *a companion publication. He writes on financial markets, trading, and options.*

TRADING PSYCHOLOGY

How Great Traders Go Bad

As traders achieve success and higher levels of profitability, they become more at risk for failure. The problem? Their egos get in the way of their success. Here's how to stay the course.

by John A. Sarkett

L ike a pilot, a police officer, or a trapeze artist, a professional trader knows he must follow the rules just to stay alive. Usually, this thought is enough to focus the mind. But occasionally, the realization is lost. Mistakes follow. Losses mount. An otherwise great trader succumbs. A great trader goes bad.

How to avoid that tragic circumstance was the subject of a recent Futures Industry Association (FIA) presentation in Chicago by professional trader and trading coach Ray Kelly. "Large traders trade more zeroes than small traders, but the process is the same," he opined.

"The catalyst for destruction," Kelly says, "is most often ego." Ego is the Ebola virus to the active trader. There is an antidote, however: humility. At the onset of paralyzing ego, humility must be administered at once, or results can be fatal. It is even more effective if administered in advance, not unlike a vaccine.

Can you or I become infected? Of course. What can be done to protect against ego and its devastating effects?

Kelly suggests paying close attention to the following four areas: self-knowledge, market knowledge, trading strategy, and risk management. Answer the hard questions for yourself before the market does it for you. Like meditation or exercise, attention must be paid each day for maximum effectiveness.

SELF-KNOWLEDGE

First, when you come in the door to your trading room, leave your ego outside. Kelly defines ego as the sense of who we believe we are: a trader, a religious person, a parent, a spouse.

When the overinflated ego gains the throne, rules go out the door. Egotism consumes natural and healthy caution, replacing it with an illusion of invincibility. An overdeveloped ego fells even the most successful, sometimes *especially* the most successful trader.

The trapeze artist, expecting occasional failure, practices with a net. He knows that he is not more durable than the concrete below. He knows that he can only exist in the high-flying environment by following the rules.

The trouble is, ego is not software that can be easily reinstalled in the trader psyche. It is hardware. We are hardwired with ego. Ego is self-identity. The ego never wants to be ignored, left out, or left behind. But sometimes it gets out of control and becomes self-absorbed and unrealistic. Sometimes you have to decide not to run with the crowd. But to do so, you have to go against your wiring.

There is something in humans that wants to believe in the hero, the guru, the champion, and for many, to become that person. If you can't, it is almost as good to run with him or her — a dream come true! Usually, though, you can't. You can only watch the hero from the stands.

But in the financial markets, you have the opportunity to participate directly or partner with the prospective hero. His glory becomes your glory. This prospect is so appealing, it will cause some of us to leave sense, common or otherwise, far behind.

WATCH OUT!

In the 1980s, I participated in a risk arbitrage–managed account program run by a major brokerage firm, supposedly run by supertraders. Ascending to the hero's podium, my account executive disclosed that returns were expected to be 60% to 100%, but if only mediocre returns were generated, the return might be as low as 30%.

Hundreds of trades (and commissions) later, I went through the laborious task of reconstructing the trading history and actual return of my account. It was 12%, exactly the money market rate of the day.

Contrast the swashbuckling image of the wanna-be trading hero with the wry comment of a master trader: "We know we don't know what we're doing."

Far from true — the comment was in reference to the fact that we can't predict rate cuts, market movements, or the future in general — but it contrasts starkly with those offering spectacular returns and is undoubtedly a better and safer way to navigate the treacherous waters of the markets. One solid trading methodology is to take trend-following positions across many markets, expecting a few large gains to outweigh numerous losses.

DEFINING SUCCESS

While the psyche is often looking for others to admire and emulate, it is not taking the time and effort to define success for itself. No, it is easier and more fun to soak up the reflected light from the hero or try to be one yourself.

What *is* success? For speaker Ray Kelly, success has been earning 40% returns each year, with no drawdowns, and having ample time with his family, he says.

HOW DO I PREPARE?

WHO AM I, WHY DO I TRADE?

WHAT ARE MY BELIEFS?

The MARKET IS NEVER WRONG

DOUG TILLER

To define your own success, you must answer these questions:

- Who am I?
- Why do I trade?
- How do I prepare?
- What are my beliefs about myself? About trading?
- Am I ready to handle the pressures of trading?

Sound too easy? Have you actually *done* it? Kelly observes:

"Great truths unfold at the level of the student. As a student learns more, these questions become deeper and more profound."

Ray Kelly's own introspection included working through a family background of an alcoholic father, and a religious upbringing. The religious upbringing instituted the idea that it was evil to be rich. The instability in his home made him feel that the tension and insecurity was somehow his fault, and therefore, he was not worthy of success. These powerful subconscious beliefs limited his success until he worked through them. When he resolved his own conflicts, he was able to progress to a higher level of trading success.

Do these subconscious messages really sabotage your trading? There is evidence that indicates that this may be the case. Kelly mentions a university study that indicates a high degree of unresolved guilt among prisoners. The study con-

> **Small losses are better than large ones. Keep losses predetermined and small. At best, professional traders are right 50% of the time or less, so they must take only small losses.**

cludes that prisoners committed crimes so that external activity would match internal guilt, not the other way around.

Other enemies of trading success: divorce, employment change, trauma, illness, or anything that creates emotional distractions or pain.

Not only that, "If you owned a Testarossa, you wouldn't think anything of having it checked and tuned on a regular basis," Kelly points out. "Many trader egos are too big for a regular tuneup."

What to do? Often, you do not realize you are laboring under the weight of conflict. It shows up as poor performance or an inability to follow your own rules. Losses are the inevitable byproduct. What to do? It depends on the person and the severity of the problem. The best course is to do regular introspection exercises. Know the resources you need before you need them. If you are already in the fire? Walk away. Take time off. Get counseling. Don't trade in the markets until your conflicts are resolved. Do not make the expensive mistake of thinking it will go away if you ignore it.

Other questions to ask yourself about your state of mind, Kelly cites, are:

- Do others comment on my personality traits negatively?
- Do I suffer extremes in emotions?
- Is my body sending me a message?
- Am I uncomfortable with this subject?
- Do I take responsibility for my actions?

"Society teaches us to externalize our failures," Kelly opines. "Bad system. Bad broker. Bad quotes. Introspection is just too painful." But to be a successful trader, you must go against the grain and do the heavy lifting of introspection.

APPROACH THE MARKETS WITH EQUANIMITY

Incorporating a "bottlecap" mentality in your trading is best, Ray Kelly suggests. Like on the TV sitcom *Laverne & Shirley* at the brewery, you put one bottlecap on after another, and then you go home and plan your excitement—*after* work. He recommends that you don't seek excitement from the markets, or unhappily, you may find it.

Similarly, $1.5 billion Chesapeake Capital chief executive officer and former Turtle Trader R. Jerry Parker says trading is a brick-upon-brick enterprise, but that commodity trading advisor (CTA) clients prefer a "rock star" approach, adding, "They want magic."

Trading in some 70 of the most liquid 150 futures markets, patiently seeking breakouts, the Chesapeake system is a technical, trend-following system. The system will generate 200 trades per year, of which some six will pay for losses and generate returns, he explains. Obviously, if you invest too much negative emotion in the 194 losers, it's likely you won't be around for the six big winners.

MARKET KNOWLEDGE

Market knowledge is the second major pillar you must depend on to avoid a market catastrophe. You must ask yourself regularly:

- What affects markets?
- How might things be changing?
- When do you know you are wrong?
- What are you trying to extract from them?

Part of market knowledge is defining how much you expect to make in the markets. If you're a typical newcomer, you may be looking to double your money. For a pro like Jerry Parker, the answer is much more modest. His goal: 2% per month.

YOUR TRADING SYSTEM

Develop your trading system. For Chesapeake Capital, the system is rule-based, trend-following, and diversified, no bias short or long. "This flies in the face of what clients want: graduates of fancy schools, huge research budgets, an intuitive approach on what's going to happen before it happens," Parker says. "Obviously, you can't know what's going to happen before it happens, and maybe an interest rate cut is the start of a major trend, and maybe it's okay to get in after. That's our approach."

Kelly also advises traders to develop a trading system they can succeed with, one geared to their own personality and financial means. "If you have abstract ideas of what you want and how you are going to accomplish it, that is what you will get, an abstract result," he insists. Test your system, he goes on to say. What are the characteristics of the system? Is it consistent? Do you understand why it works? Does it work in all markets? Does it fit your personality? Then attend to business: Do your homework every night. Your competitors do. Determine your answers the night before the market does.

MANAGE RISK

Fourth, and most important, you must *manage* risk. No matter

---

INSIGHT INTO TRADING TECHNIQUES

Former accountant R. Jerry Parker, head of Chesapeake Capital, spoke to the FIA gathering on industry considerations as befits his position with the $1.5 billion trading company. His address covered topics such as commodity trading advisor vs. hedge funds, client relations, and the rise of electronic exchanges. He also answered some questions, where attendees were able to gain insight into his firm's trading techniques. His answers were short and direct:

On markets: "There to fool people."

On neural nets: "Learning from the last trades? Not effective for us. Markets are always changing."

On trading systems: "Methodologies have degraded over time. It is getting tougher to develop a successful system."

On countertrend trading: "The reason for it is a lot of traders as well as clients don't like trend-following. It's not intuitive, not natural, too long-term, not exciting enough."

On gamesmanship: "I must protect myself from those looking for my stops. … I have to be a better gamesman than that. Go ahead and look for my stops; you won't find them."

On victims of recent market disasters: "They said, 'The market's wrong, it'll come back.' The market is never wrong."

On day-to-day trading: "Probably my best technique is not picking up the phone to close out a winning trade."

On his background as a Turtle Trader: "Having a mentor is important. It's important to live with someone who says, 'It's okay to lose money.'"

On advice to young traders: "Get a mentor. You're in it for the long haul."

• Ray Kelly is a veteran trader, financial consultant, and seminar speaker. He can be reached via www.brisas.com or www.tradersoasis.com.
• R. Jerry Parker is CEO of Chesapeake Capital, Richmond, VA. More on Parker may be found at http://turtletrader.com/jerryparker.html.
• Jerry Kopf is a partner in Benjamin & Jerold Discount Stock & Options Brokers of Chicago. He may be reached via E-mail: kopf@earthlink.net.

—J.S.

---

how great your knowledge of yourself and the markets are, and how sound your system is, if you don't manage risk, you won't last.

Kelly avers that the successful, long-term trader must answer a few questions, the first of which is: How much risk per trade? Various traders risk 0.5% to 5% of capital per trade. This figure must be fit into your system.

Next, do I *understand* my risk? Where are my stops, and what do they mean? Risk must be quantified. Is my system discretionary or systematic? A systematic approach takes all signals generated by a trading system. A discretionary system allows the trader to make exceptions to what he buys or sells within the framework of the signals he generates. And losses are expected. You are not a bad trader if they occur.

As Chicago options discount broker Jerry Kopf puts it: "It's okay to *be* wrong. It's not okay to *stay* wrong." In fact, Kelly makes a distinction between what some people refer to as "drawdowns" and what he refers to as "losses." "A drawdown is a loss taken within a defined strategy. It is *part* of the strategy. If you do not have a strategy, then it's just a loss. Traders misname the loss in hopes to deceive themselves." A drawdown is not a personal statement about *you*, it is an expected part of the business plan.

Are you unwilling to take a small loss? Small losses are better than large ones. Keep losses predetermined and small. At best, professional traders are right 50% of the time or less, so they must take only small losses. A few large ones would put them out of business, and the goal is to stay in business. "Money management is crucial," Kelly says. "This is why the exchanges have revolving doors — for those who don't master this critical skill."

Kelly notes that when losses start piling up, amateurs increase bet size, but professionals decrease bet size. Don't try to catch up on one trade. If your system is sound, it will make money over time. You *will* recapture losses over time. And that's okay, because you are looking for 3-5% a month, as Kelly does, not a fast double-play.

TWO LAST QUESTIONS

Two last questions to ask yourself as a market participant: Am I profitable, and am I as profitable as I could be? If not, why not, and how can I change? Ray Kelly concludes with one message: "If you want to keep getting what you're getting, keep doing what you're doing."

Like the pilot, policeman and trapeze artist, you follow the rules of the game and respect the rules of the game. You respect the boundaries, you respect how hard the concrete is and how soft you are, and so you survive. The alternative is too costly.

John A. Sarkett writes on and trades in the financial markets. He is the developer of Option Wizard software.

†*See Traders' Glossary for definition*

S&C

The MARKET IS NEVER WRONG

The Official Journal for Personal Investing
Originally published FEBRUARY 2008. SFO magazine. **SFO**

Go East Future Traders, Go East!

First he rode all over Asia on his motorcycle looking for investment opportunities and wrote a best-seller about it (1995). Next he married his travel companion, fathered a child and educated his young daughter in Mandarin and English. Then, attracting considerable notice, investment biker and adventure capitalist Jimmy Rogers sold his New York townhouse and moved to China. That was two years ago.

Signs of the times. Since then, many have been following this modern-day Marco Polo, operationally at least, if not physically. Including American futures traders, especially those who don't mind, or even prefer, working at night.

Although U.S. markets are flagging in the face of the subprime and collateralized-debt-obligation crisis, Asian markets are nothing less than white hot.

HKEX: Access to China

If you want exposure to mainland China stocks, the Hong Kong Futures Exchange (HKEx) accommodates, and it is doing a land office business. Volume in all futures and options had increased 114 percent as 2007 drew to a close, (options

By John A. Sarkett

66

161 percent, futures 63 percent), according to exchange officials. To put this in perspective, U.S. options volume grew 38 percent for the same period. HKEx's most active products are stock options, stock index futures and stock index options.

The most actively traded contracts include Hang Seng Index (HSI) futures and options, mini-HSI futures, H shares Index futures and options. H shares are shares of mainland China companies listed on the HKEx. The Hong Kong Exchange offers options on H-share stocks, including China Life, Industrial and Commercial Bank of China, Bank of China, and PetroChina.

What's on the horizon? Possibly a mini-H shares Index futures contract to provide an efficient trading and hedging tool for retail investors. Market demand is there: HKEx officials note the size of the H shares Index futures contract is several times its original size as a result of the sharp increase in the index's level during the past few years. The contract multiplier for H shares Index futures is $50, and the index level at rollout was about 4,000. So it began as a $200,000 contract, but today its level is approximately 16,900 for an $845,000 value!

Taiwan Up 112 percent Per Year

The Taiwan Futures Exchange (TAIFEX) was established in 1997, with its first futures contract traded in 1998 and its first options contract traded in 2001. At the exchange, growth has been similarly heady: Between 2001 and 2006, the volume exploded 112 percent compounded annually for all contracts traded, including stock index futures, stock index options, stock options, interest rate futures and metal futures (gold).

Not satisfied with this moonshot growth rate, administrators at TAIFEX have launched a major push to attract more volume through foreign participation. TAIFEX plans new products to further entice foreign business including currency, short-term interest rate, mini gold and volatility index futures. TAIFEX has also lowered margins for day traders and has established a futures market maker system, along with a futures spread margining system.

As of Oct. 31, with a total of 1.162 million accounts opened, 99.45 percent were opened by retail investors, though growth has leveled off since 2004—which is one reason TAIFEX officials are looking abroad for new business. Picking up the slack, institutional accounts have steadily increased in trading size to gain the upper hand in market share, most recently tallied at 63 percent institutional and 37 percent retail.

Leading institutions at TAIFEX include familiar names such as Merrill Lynch Futures, Citigroup, UBS and J.P. Morgan. Expect that number to grow.

CME Group Links with Seoul

U.S. exchanges are joining hands with their foreign counterparts to widen access to Asian markets for U.S. futures traders.

CME recently added KOSPI 200 futures from the Korea Exchange to their Globex platform. The KOSPI 200 contract trades from 2 a.m. to 3 p.m. Central time, which is 5 p.m. to 6 a.m. Seoul time.

CME Group Executive Chairman Terry Duffy called it an "important part of our continued global expansion."

Broker's Perspective: 'Two-sided Affair'

The futures world is moving—and moving quickly—to Asia says Steve M. Kelsey, CFA, CMT, managing director, Interactive Brokers LLC (IB), who spoke via telephone from his offices in Hong Kong.

"The more savvy U.S. traders are definitely showing increased interest in Asian futures, particularly Nikkei and Hang Seng Index futures," he says. "And sometime soon, we will see a new contract from China as well—the Chinese Shanghai Shenzhen 300 Index futures—which will increase interest further."

Kelsey thinks that the launch of index futures on the Shanghai Futures Exchange will increase demand for equity index futures in the region. "While overseas investors will not be able to access this market immediately due to Chinese regulations, they can trade the Hang Seng China Enterprise Index futures (H share futures) listed in Hong Kong," he says. This index tracks the major Chinese companies that are listed on HKEx.

Kelsey continues, "Whereas U.S. markets used to lead Asian markets, now it is a more two-sided affair and Asian markets often lead U.S. markets, so traders are positioning themselves via these contracts overnight before the U.S. session opens. This is particularly evident after the weekend, as Asian markets generally open first so [traders] can react to the weekend news [more quickly]. Globalization has indeed come to the futures markets for the U.S. retail trader."

What caveats does the IB managing director raise for new Asian futures traders based in the USA?

"Just the typical ones," he says. "Know your exchange rules, holidays, hours of trading—that sort of thing. Every once in a while, we get a call from a trader 'screaming murder' about not being able to trade Hong Kong markets because the 'platform is down,' when it turns out Hong Kong is on holiday. There are some other local customs as well, for example, the 'no bust' rule at the Japanese exchanges for options. If you make an error, back in the U.S. you can sometimes break a trade, say if you [enter] 900 instead of 9. Not in Japan. So take extra precaution [and] review your trade carefully before you push 'buy' or 'sell.'"

Summarizing Asian futures for the retail trader, Kelsey says, "In a word, growth. China's the place. Chinese investors and traders are presently somewhat restricted, but their ranks will grow in time. And liquidity will explode."

It takes time and effort to break into a new environment, but Kelsey says for those who aspire to master global markets, Asia is the place to begin.

Faster growth, More Attractive Opportunities

President and CEO of newly formed Gateway Capital LLC (in Chicago). Matt Trapani was traveling in China when he answered my questions by e-mail.

For Americans interested in trading Asian futures, he says, "I believe you need to first take a macro-economic view of Asia. To begin with, there are many emerging markets that are growing much faster than most continents'

[economies together]. As a result, there is more capital, trading and volatility—very attractive attributes for traders in the USA. In addition, with the advent of electronic trading and the Internet, the world of trading has no boundaries. So access to the markets is fast, reliable and secure."

With some 10 percent of its business in Asian futures, his firm serves a number of active traders in Asian futures. He expects this number to grow dramatically as Asian markets (especially Chinese) become freely accessible to U.S. investors in the months and years ahead.

Most popular contracts originate, he says, at the Singapore, Hong Kong, Korean and Japanese exchanges.

In addition to these major established markets, traders are asking for and developments are taking place to create new markets for India and, of course, China.

Who makes a good candidate to trade Asian futures? "Traders who understand the correlations between markets," Trapani says. "Asian markets are really no different than any other market—in light of both profit potential and various risks, including political and currency."

Drawbacks? "The time-zone difference is always an issue to consider," he says. "Hong Kong, for example, is 14 hours ahead of the Central time zone, so it is a night-shift enterprise in the U.S."

Concerning the future of Asian futures for American retail traders, Trapani says "Over time, more and more Asian markets will become part of the global trading environment for [those] traders seeking [to] access new opportunities, with availability any time of the day or location."

India: Stirring Slowly

Speaking at a meeting of the Futures Industry Association in Chicago during November, Patrick J. Catania, head, international relations, National Commodities and Derivatives Exchange (NCDEX), said that the Mumbai exchange is presently mired in a "regulatory quagmire."

He cited as evidence the recent banning of wheat futures there because officials deemed that trading these contracts "caused inflation." The situation went from bad to worse. Without a pricing mechanism, farmers withheld their product from the market, and prices climbed another 30 percent to 40 percent.

Nevertheless, when Indian officials come to terms with the role of futures, Catania expects NCDEX to take its place among the leaders of emerging markets. His best guess: approximately three years from now.

"Is it worth watching, waiting for?" he poses the rhetorical question. "With 300 million affluent, middle-class Indians who save 31 percent of their annual income (compared to U.S. savers who recently were saving -1 percent of their annual incomes), indeed it is. India will be a player. Be ready. The potential is vast."

Latest Developments

The China Securities Regulatory Commission (CSRC) in November approved two leading futures brokers to purchase stakes in two Chinese brokerages: J.P. Morgan Broking (Hong Kong) Limited put up $3.29 million for a 49 percent stake in China's Zhongshan Futures, and Calyon Financial Hong Kong Limited laid out $5.64 million for a 42 percent share of China's CITIC Futures.

More such transactions will follow, but foreigners will not be permitted to own controlling shares, according to the CSRC.

No Comment

Nevertheless, perhaps one of the best indications of the sharpness of the cutting-edge of Asian futures is the high number of brokerage firms that turned down my request for comment. They cited a lack of capability or lack of expertise as their reason.

Asian futures markets are still quite new. So if you aren't trading them, you haven't missed out by any means. And the meeting room at FIA? Less than one-quarter full.

But the times, as Bob Dylan said, "they are a changin'," and with ever-increasing velocity. With one of the world's premier new firms choosing Hong Kong as its IPO debut location, with a new Chinese stock index in the wings ready to come on stage and be traded, and right behind it the dam of Chinese (and Indian) investor-traders ready to burst on the world

scene, I doubt, should SFO revisit this theme in five years, that will still be the case.

Although some analysts predict a Chinese market crash before then (and perhaps just as quickly a recovery), by 2013 the Shenzhen 300 Stock Index may just be as widely quoted as the Dow 30 or the S&P 500, at least on the world scene, if not on CNBC's American edition.

And in 10 or so years? My guess is that Jimmy Rogers, who will then be a spry 75, will have not yet come home to Gotham as fresh opportunities in Asia continue to abound.

John A. Sarkett created Option Wizard® software, Option-Wizard.com. He is the author of *Extraordinary Comebacks: 201 Inspiring Stories of Courage, Triumph, and Success* (2007), and is finishing *Monthly Income Strategies with Options: Adjusting Your Position to Earn Significant, Steady Yields.*

BACK TO SCHOOL:
Choosing Your Options Mentor

Online trading continues to grow by leaps and bounds, but consistent profitability? Elusive as ever for many. Now, however, a growing minority of options traders are breaking through—thanks to their mentors or coaches.

The mentor movement is new and growing. I found no widely accepted distinction between terms across the industry; one person's coach is another's mentor. The transaction is simple: You pay me; I'll teach you how to trade. From there, the variations in style and delivery are endless.

By John A. Sarkett

So how many people have a mentor? Thinkorswim brokerage founder Tom Sosnoff estimates the figure is 1 percent to 2 percent of active options traders. "These are the 'A' students," he says, "and it's paying off for them."

I can only survey the scene here, but I've learned enough to be convinced there are some real nuggets of gold to be had, but some mines are richer and yield more instructional "gold" than others. Use this piece as a catalyst to get acquainted with the burgeoning field and to seek out those mentors who were invariably missed despite my best efforts. (This booming cottage industry attracts new entrants each month.)

Here's the essential proposition: If you think education is expensive, try ignorance. Or as one coach put it: If you get just one profitable idea, it will be worth many times the fee paid over time. (And sometimes you don't have to pay anything. More on that later.)

IN THE BEGINNING

One of the first mentors appeared on the scene more than 25 years ago: Van K. Tharp, Ph.D., head of the International Institute of Trading Mastery (IITM.com).

Having coached traders for 15-plus years by the time he wrote *Trade Your Way to Financial Freedom* in 1999 and having interviewed thousands, it can be said that no one knows the trader's psyche more deeply. In his best seller, Tharp raises important issues: the right trading system, personality matching, position sizing. However, he doesn't pick your trades for you or model a portfolio over time, even though many mentors do. After 25 years in the business, he is busier than ever; when I checked in at IITM, he had just returned from a two-month international speaking and seminar tour.

Another early mentor, Dr. Alexander Elder, is a bestselling author and seminar provider. He had the charming habit of following up with small groups of campers at odd times over the year in his New York City apartment. When the business at hand was completed, the practicing psychiatrist and his troops would decamp for a special meal at one of New York's finest and/or most interesting restaurants. He kept the relationships going—that's what mentors do. Presently, Dr. Elder (Elder. com) refers would-be mentees to his former student Kerry Lovvorn (KerryLovvorn.com).

NEXT GENERATION: SOFTWARE PLUS

Although they may not have been first, most credit the folks at OptionVue software (OptionVue.com) for starting the most visible mentoring program (2004)— one that first used webinar technology that is now omnipresent. Presently, Steve Lentz leads a team of DiscoverOptions mentors who teach the full range of delta-neutral strategies, but also touch on something few others do: futures options. Lentz makes the point that futures options often operate conversely to stock and index options (think: oil up, stocks down), so when added to a portfolio, futures options can smooth results.

OptionVue mentees have the added benefit of being coached on the fine points of the OptionVue platform, and there are many. Students pay $6,000 to join the program and about the same for the software itself, plus or minus depending on the services chosen. Despite the huge advances in software offered by brokerage firms (free on their platforms), many still choose OptionVue as the "gold standard" of options analysis software and don't mind paying for it. In a touch of convergence, OptionVue itself added brokerage services to its suite of offerings in August 2008.

Dan Sheridan, a 22-year Chicago Board Options Exchange veteran, helped create the OptionVue mentoring program but left to start his own mentoring service (SheridanMentoring.com). He specializes in monthly income delta-neutral strategies, attracting a particularly active and loyal band of partisans from around the world. Some are advanced students such as Dan Harvey, a 14-year veteran of successful condor trading, who occasionally takes the mike to teach as well. Sheri-

"Mentoring to me means a service that can guide you to success."

dan has a team of full-time mentors to assist him, most with CBOE backgrounds and a bevy of guest speakers from all corners of the options world.

All teaching is archived on his website (some 3,000 webinars as of this writing), where students share comments, spreadsheets and ideas. Sheridan's fee is $6,000. Pay and you're in "for life" and can listen to live webinars eight-plus hours a day, five or six days a week. Sheridan also holds an annual face-to-face convention in Chicago for his students; a high percentage attend. Results? Some of his best students are regularly earning 70 percent to 100 percent annualized returns.

THE DELTA FORCE

Like Sheridan, a number of other mentors specialize more or less in delta-neutral options strategies. "Delta" means change, hence "change-neutral" strategies—if you will. These strategies make money if the market doesn't move—too much or too fast. These include calendar spreads, double calendars, double diagonals, butterflies and the increasingly popular condor.

With a staff of three, Jared Woodard runs Condor Options.com. He started mentoring in 2007 and currently teaches some 300 traders. Woodward and the other traders blog on the market daily, with touches of Jon Stewart, Stephen Colbert and Dan Rather from time to time. The site offers a newsletter, real-time sample iron condor-options trades and access to support staff. They employ exchange-traded funds (ETFs) as the underlying of their iron condors in order to benefit from the tighter spreads and enhanced liquidity that ETFs offer. Woodard emphasizes risk management and careful asset allocation. A believer in openness and transparency, he publishes every trade made in the newsletter on the website. CondorOptions.com charges $139 per month, $749 per six months or $1,339 per year.

Another delta-neutral specialist is Market Neutral Options (MarketNeutralOptions.com), run by Gary Ang of Singapore. If "learn by watching" is a valid category of mentoring, and I think it is, then advisory services such as this one qualify as mentors, especially as defined by Ang.

"Mentoring to me means a service that can guide you to success. Not just a one-time lecture, mentoring gives me the feel of a more personal touch, like a hand-holding, step-by-step coach who is always by your side to provide advice," he says. Ang achieves this with his advisory newsletter but with an unusual twist.

"The special aspect of my service is that the subscribers only pay for advisories that make money. Simply put, if my recommendations don't make money, the subscribers don't have to pay a cent. To make a good deal even better, the maximum fee for any month is capped at $50," he says.

Ang mainly employs market-neutral options strategies such as iron condors and double diagonals and trades only indexes such as the S&P 500 Index, Russell 2000 Index and index-tracking ETFs including SPDR S&P 500 Index, iShares Russell 2000 Index or Dow Diamonds.

Closer to home is the not-so-widely known but wildly successful Mike Parnos (who occasionally contributes to SFO). Parnos has been teaching traders for 15 years, and his claim to fame is a trading record that has been profitable for 59 of the last 64 months. You can read some of Parnos' excellent writings (part of his diverse business background includes communications) at Mike-Parnos.com. He also writes a column twice a week called The Couch Potato Trader for Option Investor.com, which suggests trades for a monthly port-

SFOMAG.COM!

Read an excerpt from John Sarkett's November 2008 SFO article detailing what Dan Harvey has learned from 14 years of trading condors.

folio. Additionally, Parnos teaches two-day advanced seminars five to six times a year for $895 to $995 per seminar; repeaters attend free.

One of Parnos' brightest students is now a mentor (since 2005) and has a catchy name meant to convey fierce risk management: the Options Linebacker, otherwise known as Craig Severson (OptionsLinebacker.com). It's easy to put on a trade, Severson says, but how you defend it from there is the key. He has been investing in the market since 1996 and now trades for a living in addition to mentoring. Severson holds two degrees in electrical engineering and an MBA. He spent 19 years in telecommunications and is a junior college instructor in business and economics. Severson says explaining difficult topics in a simple manner is his passion and has a healthy respect for mitigating risk.

Severson uses webinars, newsletters ($49 per month), seminars ($249) and phone one-on-ones. He focuses on the iron condor, using vertical credit spreads on index options or index ETF options, as well as uses butterflies and delta-neutral hedges for risk management. Also, Severson features swing-based futures trades to take advantage of trending conditions that are not optimal for the iron condor.

Another business-accomplished individual, having created and sold a company before he delved into the world of options, is John Ondercin (OptionsMentoring.com). He is a been-there, done-that kind of guy who doesn't waste a student's time. "I teach a method that gets new traders out the door and making money within their first or second month of trading," Ondercin says.

"We find that many of our students, maybe 65 percent, need a paradigm change in the way they think about options. In my methodology, naked option writing and trades like covered calls are too risky, and time after time, I see people lose their trading accounts with these strategies. I teach risk management, money management and high-probability trading."

After going through Ondercin's instructional DVDs, beginner and advanced, the student calls Ondercin for a one-on-one personal consultation. This is all for a one-time fee of $3,500. So does it work? Ondercin claims an average of 62 percent annual return on his own option trading and many satisfied clients.

Author, co-founder and software designer of thinkorswim (though no longer with thinkorswim), Charles Cottle is a mentor who focuses on range-style positioning, including verticals, wing spreads, calendars and hybrid combinations of these. Additionally, he employs a proprietary technical analysis tool called Diamonetrics™.

Cottle's market roots run deep, including stints at the CBOE, Chicago Board of Trade, Chicago Mercantile Exchange and thinkorswim. Over the years, he has trained a number of market luminaries including Chuck Whitman who started as a soybean options trader and went on to create and manage Infinium Capital Management. (Whitman has sent some 40 traders and programmers to Cottle for instruction.)

"It is important to encourage the fact that one can be wrong and do something about it early on," he says. "Having the consciousness of 'What would I do here, right now, in the market if I had no position?' is vital for life-long trading success. I work to apply creative adjustments to avoid having losing positions fester."

Self mentoring programs begin at $25 per hour (RiskDoctor.com) and his RD4U (personal consultation) is priced at $3,240 and starts with a questionnaire. For second opinions or other coaching, there is a charge of $18 per minute on a retainer basis. In addition, Cottle offers to speak personally to prospects regarding an appropriate game plan for up to 15 minutes at no charge.

THE EDUCATION FIRMS

In addition to soloists such as Parnos, Severson, Ondercin et al., and smaller firms like Condor Options, larger firms also own substantial real estate along Mentor Boulevard.

With 19 offices around the world, the Online Trading Academy (TradingAcademy.com) qualifies as one of these. The company, which started in June 1997, boasts some 8,000 graduates—many have gone on to significant careers in the markets. The Chicago office's director of

73

> If you think education is expensive, try ignorance.

trading, Craig Weil, says, "Our Extended Learning Track (XLT) online classes offer four basic learning environments for stocks, forex and futures. OTA teaches many different trading strategies and emphasizes the importance of learning different trading skills, practicing those skills with live trading and building a personalized trading plan customized to your individual needs as a trader." XLT programs are $6,000 for three months, and $500 per month thereafter; unlimited access can be purchased for $10,000.

The 26 Online Trading Academy instructors are former professional traders, brokers and market makers, and all still actively trade their own accounts. "Staff must have at least five documented years of trading experience and must continue to be active in the markets to qualify for instructor certification. Each has a specialty as well," Weil says.

In the options world, the 800-pound gorilla in the room remains Optionetics (Optionetics.com), the company that took seminars to a whole 'nother level back in the 1990s. They pioneered the options infomercial, advertising free preview workshops, which would then include an invitation to the basic $2,000 to $3,000 seminar. These delta-neutral seminars were typically followed by more advanced and more expensive seminars teaching strategies with intriguing names such as the "Tarzan-and-Jane" spread, and often in more appealing locales than back home—Las Vegas for example.

The company was (and is) extremely successful. It claims a staggering 338,000 grads from 50 countries. For a long time, Optionetics more or less owned the options education niche. That world has since moved online, and Optionetics followed suit. Its new Optionetics Signature Series is a group of 90-minute online classes, each tackling an individual topic. Each session is presented live and recorded; these are then available to the students for 21 days after the live date. Optionetics continues to present live seminars as well.

Founder George Fontanills and his right-hand man Tom Gentile now teach only the advanced seminars for the company. Additionally, Gentile founded Profit Strategies to teach trading systems.

THE BROKERS

OptionsXpress (optionsXpress.com) has 12 coaches on board as of this writing; each a former broker or trader. Many continue to trade for their own accounts, so their ideas are fresh and live. The mentoring program at optionsXpress is customized for each student. Senior Vice President Joe Cusick cites these key components: knowledge, application, accountability, motivation and time. Fees start at $1,500.

Across town, broker thinkorswim (thinkorswim.com) invests heavily in education. That's how the company grew from a small upstart to the No. 2 options broker and "best online broker" in 2006 and 2007 as rated by Barron's. Thinkorswim is kind of the General Motors of mentoring, offering a style and price for every would-be mentee: straight-up coaches, trade desk savants, newsletter advisories, as well as free and for-pay seminars. You couldn't get away from mentoring there if you tried.

Derivatives strategist Joe Kinahan lays it out: "We have 70 coaches at Investools. (Investools acquired thinkorswim in February 2007 for $340 million.) The student is assigned to a coaching team and can call and talk to a coach at any time. The coaches will give the student unlimited time and help [him or her] in applying the logic and strategies that [the student has] been taught in order to make trades. We field some 900 phone calls a day. Students love it because it gives them a chance to bounce ideas off of someone who is familiar with their trading styles." Additionally, thinkorswim has another 40 individuals on the thinkorswim trade desk who serve as mentors.

A thinkorswim division, Red Option (RedOption.com) is an e-mail advisory offering 11 strategy styles for $20 each per month, while Options Planet (Options

> "We find that many of our students, maybe 65 percent, need a paradigm change in the way they think about options."

Planet.com) offers classes. Finally, thinkorswim offers seminars and lots of them. "We saw more than 700,000 people in the U.S. and Canada last year," Kinahan says.

No. 3 options broker Interactive Brokers (Interactive-Brokers.com) has no mentoring program per se but has extensive webinars online to teach its advanced platform.

TRAVELING MENTORS

Best-selling author of *Options as a Strategic Investment* and professional trader Lawrence G. McMillan tapped former American Stock Exchange market maker Stan Freifeld to head his custom mentoring program (OptionStrategist.com).

Freifeld is a paradox. He's a math whiz (jumping two grades in school and earning a math degree at State University of New York) and a MENSA member but is as down-to-earth as can be.

In this mentoring program, the student spends two full days with Freifeld. He starts with an audit of client expectations and develops a unique program for each individual. Next, probabilities, expectations and money management principles are covered. Volatility and trading strategies follow that. Cost is $8,995, and tuition reimbursement is a possibility via commission rebates with three nationally recognized brokers (Terra Nova, Fidelity and optionsXpress).

Another traveling mentor (and occasional SFO writer) is John Carter (TradeTheMarkets.com). He began in 2002, and his specialty is in futures, although he also covers options and stocks. At $25,000 per week, his is the highest priced program I found, but no matter, he is booked for the next 12 months. Carter currently has eight students and some 62 graduates. About half make it as full-time traders he says. Some aren't cut out; Carter even gave back the fee to one particularly unsuited individual.

"A typical program lasts one week, and we sit side by side," he says. "On the first day, I trade and they watch. On the second day, they trade and I watch. Then I update their trading plan based on the strengths and weak-nesses I see in their own trading habits. I also show them markets and setups at which I look."

Carter plunged into the markets in high school. "My father was a broker for Morgan Stanley and got me trading options. I traded during college and my first job was a financial analyst with many ups and downs before going to full-time [trading] in 1998."

FREE MENTORING

Everybody loves free stuff, and when seminars and/or mentoring services cost between $1,000 and $25,000, free can sound pretty good. At The Options Institute, some 50 free webinars are archived at CBOE.com/LearnCenter. CBOE instructors include Sheridan of Sheridan Mentoring, CBOE's Jim Bittman, OptionVue's Lentz and TradeKing's Brian Overby, among others.

SO WHAT?

It is all well and good that mentors say their services are valuable, but what do their fee-paying students say?

I street surveyed a number of mentees (from names supplied by mentors) and found a high degree of satisfaction. I even received words like "epiphany" and "life changing."

Boil it down: Market mentors are making a difference, and for many, it's a big one. They are creating real value for the early adopting 1 percent to 2 percent who employ them. We should see their programs, ranks and numbers of protégés grow like wildfire in the months ahead.

John A. Sarkett is designer of Option Wizard® software (http://option-wizard.com) and the author of the best-selling *Extraordinary Comebacks: 201 Inspiring Stories of Courage, Triumph, and Success*. Sarkett writes frequently for financial publications and is currently working on two books *Market Mentors* and *Monthly Income Strategies from Options*.

Optimize Your IRA with Options

May 2010
By John A. Sarkett

There was a time when index and equity options traders were regarded as high-octane, win-or-lose-a-fortune types or nerdy rocket scientists. Brokers dubbed options "risky" and said "stay away." Now, however, more and more investors are using options for their original purpose: to hedge risk and enhance returns.

DEFINING RISK

Brokerages spell this out in their materials. For example, thinkorswim writes, "There are limitations, restrictions, and tax implications in connection with the use of options as an investment strategy in a retirement account such as an IRA [individual retirement account]. We do not allow for short stock, naked short calls or futures."

Another options brokerage, optionsXpress, puts it this way: "We allow trading of equity and index options in IRAs based on the trading level assigned to an investor. Trading in IRAs includes call buying, put buying, cash-secured put writing, spreads, and covered calls."

Again, these are all risk-defined strategies—no naked (uncovered) short calls or naked short puts (not backed by cash or securities) that could decimate an account.

So, with these caveats accounted for, how does one get started in a risk-controlled, risk-defined manner? Below are three strategies to consider.

SELL PUTS AGAINST CASH

Say you have researched and followed XYZ stock, which is $100 per share. Its prospects are good, and it pays a significant dividend. You want to own the stock, but would like to get it at a discount. You can sell the $90 put one, three or 12 months into the future. This gives you the obligation to purchase the stock at $90 between the time you sell the put option and its expiration date.

What if XYZ stays at $100 or goes higher? You would keep the premium if XYZ stays above $90—the amount for which you sold the option—and enhance your return by the amount of the premium.

On the other hand, if XYZ dropped below $90, you would still be obligated to purchase it at $90 or buy back your put (now at a loss) between now and expiration.

So it works both ways. The key: You are willing to own XYZ at $90. A short put has the same risk curve as a covered call: a capped upside against an unlimited downside. But the downside is covered here with cash, which is why a broker allows you to use this strategy in a retirement account.

COLLAR YOUR STOCK

If you did purchase XYZ at $90 but are concerned that the entire market or XYZ stock could fall soon, wiping out the fat dividend and more, you can use options to establish a collar. A collar is when you buy an $85 put in this example and to finance it, sell a $95 call.

If the stock goes to zero, you can still "put" the stock to the put seller at $85 between now and expiration. The tradeoff: If the stock increases, your gain is capped at $95, where you sold the call.

A collar can be a long-term or temporary strategy. The "width" of the collar is determined by how much risk you are willing to take.

SELL CALLS ON YOUR STOCK

The most basic options strategy is selling calls, a strategy that fits well in an IRA.

For example, XYZ has moved from $90 to $110 in a short period. You feel the stock is now nearly fully priced but may have just a bit more to run, so you sell a 90-day $120 call option and the cash premium is deposited into your account.

If the XYZ price is more than $120 at expiration, the stock is called away from you (you sell it at the agreed-upon $120). But if you would rather keep the stock, you can buy back the call (perhaps at more than you sold it). You still would earn a profit due to the gain on the stock from the $110 level where you sold the call.

You could also "roll" your option. That is buy the call you sold, sell another 30-day or 90-day call or longer contract at the same $120 strike or higher.

The main point to understand is that you are still in control. Options give you, well ... options. But always at a cost. Everything in options is a tradeoff between risk and reward.

ADVANCED STRATEGIES

There is much more to using options in IRAs, but selling puts and calls and placing collars are some of the basics. Options strategies can be considerably more complex and go by arcane names such as condors, butterflies and calendars. But as exotic as they are and sound, these can be put to work in IRAs as well because, in each, the risk is clearly defined.

Transaction costs should be considered when assessing the potential of such strategies. Quite simply, more legs mean more commissions. For instance, OptionsHouse brokerage had a flat rate per spread up to four legs for a while, but it changed the policy in December 2009. It now charges a flat fee plus per contract fees—at the time of this writing, $12.50 per ticket plus 15 cents per contract.

Still, the profitability of these strategies has the potential to more than make up for the increased cost.

Financial institutions such as the Chicago Board Options Exchange, brokers and private mentors provide educational programs and can take you as deep into the subject of advanced options as you wish to go. There are a number of books on the subject as well.

This story will get you started thinking about ways to cut risk and boost returns in your IRA. A wise investor needs access to every tool available, and that includes the conservative, risk-reducing and return-enhancing capabilities of options.

John A. Sarkett writes frequently for financial publications and is creator of Option Wizard® software. He is the author of Extraordinary Comebacks: 201 Inspiring Stories of Courage, Triumph, and Success; Extraordinary Comebacks 2: 250 (more) Inspiring Stories of Courage, Triumph, and Success; and Option Wizard® Trading Method.

ADVANCED POSITIONS

CALENDARS

A calendar trade is the sale of a near option against a long position in a farther-dated option (e.g. sell the June 2010 $100 call against buying a January 2011 $100 call). This is a debit transaction, meaning it costs you. Your potential loss is limited to that debit.

When June approaches, you can let the June short call expire or roll it to July to generate a credit, i.e. buy June and sell July. You do this repeatedly until January.

How far apart should the expiration months be? That depends on you, the underlying and your assessment of potential movement. There is no "right" answer.

BUTTERFLIES

A butterfly offers a superb way to speculate in a low-risk, high-return manner. It is composed of a long, short two, long position (e.g. long one $100 call, short two $110 calls, long one $120 call). Again, this is a debit position.

Butterflies are favored by many because they offer a high risk-reward ratio—often 10 or 20 times the debit. Place the two short strikes where you think the underlying will expire in order to generate the maximum pop for the money.

CONDORS

Finally, there is the mighty condor, a four-legged options animal that is really two widely spaced credit spreads. This unruly beast offers traders a nice credit (this is not free money!), plus a 67 percent to 85 percent probability of profit.

But the condor can turn and rend you with a big market move. You can lose $9 or more for every $1 credit. So risk management is paramount. Those who sell the short strikes at 10 deltas will typically roll up or exit at 20 to 30 deltas.

 Book Review
March 2009
John A. Sarkett

SHOWSTOPPING INSIGHT

I have a friend who is a highly savvy engineer and heads a successful consulting firm, but his real passion is for the markets—specifically options markets. He happens to be a thoughtful and successful trader—and has been for many years.

One of the characteristics that sets him apart is his knack of ferreting out the latest developments in the field: mainstream, esoteric or otherwise. Some years ago, he was the first, for example, to tell me about the creation of a new brokerage firm, a little company with the whimsical name thinkorswim. (Of course thinkorswim grew to become the No. 2 options brokerage, merged with another group and is now being bought for a handsome sum.)

Just recently my savvy friend told me about a new options book by Jeff Augen, someone with whom he had struck up an e-mail correspondence. Concerning the making of books regarding options, there is seemingly no end, but no matter. Since he recommended it, I was immediately interested.

I was not disappointed.

NO ORDINARY OPTIONS BOOK

The Volatility Edge in Options Trading is a brilliant and thoroughgoing presentation by a former high-ranking IBM executive and software startup CEO who suffered a terrible car accident and was forced to make a career change to recuperate (he has since recovered). Augen, who attacked his new enterprise full time, brought the same kind of rigor that served him so well at IBM and as an entrepreneur and applied it to his personal study of financial markets by employing exhaustive data mining and analysis. He spent more than 10 years developing a proprietary intellectual property portfolio of algorithms and software for the technical analysis of derivative prices. Along the way, he wrote more than 1 million lines of code.

In this hardcover volume, the author shares the fruits of his studies and experiences. He begins at—well—the beginning, covering the history of the options market, basics for beginners, problems with other options texts (e.g., lack of adjustment treatments throughout a trade with the typical notion that someone can just put on the trade and then wish/hope/pray all the way to expiration, which, as the author points out, equals gambling). He goes on to tackle problems with technical analysis, and then, the showstopper: several actionable and unique options strategies on volatility, earnings and expiration.

Speaking of actionable, specific strategies with risk management techniques, if you have read a great deal in this field, you know most options texts have none—zero, zilch, nada. A couple have one or two, and none I have encountered offers five or more. That certainly is not the problem here. So I rate the Augen text outstanding in this area. The treatments of expiration-week and expiration-day possibilities, including examples, stand out.

For an encore, he offers some interesting challenges for the math and engineering types among us. (I don't really think the average trader is going to lash together several Linux-driven PCs and data mine until the cows come home like Augen did, but who knows.)

In The Volatility Edge, the author appropriately takes to task other options books that only treat trades and trade results at expiration. Additionally, he provides trade adjustment examples (e.g., short strangle on pages 132 to 135).

Augen also presents some original thinking on ratio spreads, which are generally thought to be too risky since they are partially naked, but the author makes his case that they can, in fact, be managed and managed profitably.

DRAWBACKS

Any criticisms? I have very few. One is that the author idiosyncratically refers to a $100 credit as being "short $100." In addition, unlike some strategists who would strenuously disagree, Augen does not recommend adjusting butterflies, saying they are "best left alone until expiration." Lastly, there are no risk graphs to be found here.

With small changes, and given an either-or choice, I'd rather have Augen's incisive thinking than pretty pictures any day. All in all, I highly recommend this text.

John A. Sarkett contributes frequently to SFO. He is the creator of Option Wizard® software (http://option-wizard.com), and author of the best-selling Extraordinary Comebacks: 201 Inspiring Stories of Courage, Triumph, and Success.

SFO Magazine Department from:

http://www.sfomag.com/Trading_Options_News-Book_Review-dp257i95.aspx

Print | Close

HOT, HOT, HOT

By John A. Sarkett

A few years ago, risk curves were all the rage in options trading, and famous seminar givers unveiled and exhibited them with great pride.

Times have changed. Now the new wow in webinars and seminars is trading by the Greeks. If you need to get up to speed on this, author Dan Passarelli has created a great introduction for you: *Trading Option Greeks*.

With some seven years as a CBOE trader under his belt, he knows whereof he speaks. In fact, Passarelli brings a market maker's mentality to every page (i.e., managing risk, not just making profits).

His perspectives and commentaries on the highly popular delta neutral game, which is roughly equivalent to volatility trading— whether participants realize this or not—is worth the price of the text alone.

In the meat of the book, Passarelli walks the reader through various strategies and takes into account the changing nature of delta, gamma, vega and theta. For some traders, this is second nature, but for others these insights will be revelatory.

Be aware: This book is not a primer on how or when to trade, but rather a discussion of every facet of some of the most common monthly income strategies. The author establishes a mindset. Although there is not necessarily a right or wrong here, Passarelli provides a thoroughgoing discussion of everything that could go right and everything that could go wrong, plus how the ever-changing Greeks show this.

It is easy to put on a trade and easy, too, to spend little time considering in advance and taking the necessary steps to prepare for all the things that can go wrong. Passarelli makes sure you do this, and that is why this book is worth reading.

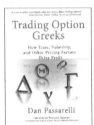
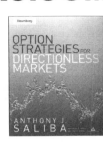
LEFT WITH QUESTIONS

Option Strategies for Directionless Markets is a comprehensive presentation of strategies, including the arcane ones with clever names such as albatross or pterodactyl; however, it has an underlying problem of always presenting strategies at expiration instead of during the trade, leaving virtually no discussion of real-time risk management techniques until the end of the text—and then only briefly.

The Q&A at the end of the book with the famous author Anthony J. Saliba, featured as a market wizard in the series by Jack D. Schwager, might have yielded some fantastic information, but just as he raises a terrific point, there is zero follow up.

An illustration: Regarding Saliba's greatest trade, Teledyne butterflies in 1984, we are not told the strikes, rather we are left to infer them from the $78 stock price and a mention that they were at the money. Saliba says, "It all started with cheap butterflies," yet later we learn that the results came not from the butterflies but from additionally accumulated out-of-the-money 85 calls that mushroomed when Teledyne was acquired for $200 per share and then went to $300 in a short squeeze. So, how cheap were the butterflies? Quantity? Which strikes? Why did he buy the out-of-the-money calls that made serious cash? We are never told the overarching strategy.

All in all, this is more of a puzzle for the Sherlock Holmes among us than a primer on sideways markets. The authors obviously have the goods, which is why it is so frustrating; they only needed the right editor to painstakingly ask all the right questions and fill in the many holes.

John A. Sarkett contributes frequently to SFO. He is the creator of Option Wizard® software (http://Option-Wizard.com) and author of the best-selling book *Extraordinary Comebacks: 201 Inspiring Stories of Courage, Triumph, and Success* (Sarkett.com).

Book Review
October 2009
John A. Sarkett

TRAINING AT A DISCOUNT

As one of the original Market Wizards (from Jack Schwager's bestselling series), Anthony J. Saliba became a trading rock star.

After winning his fortune, a good chunk of it from a Teledyne trade where the 85 calls he bought for $1 exploded in value to more than $200, he eventually left trading to found the International Trading Institute Ltd. in 1989. He also manages LiquidPoint LLC, an electronic trading solutions company.

Via ITI, Saliba and his staff have trained approximately 5,000 traders around the world on the ins and outs of options and other derivatives.

The cost of training like this is typically in the thousands, but for just $38.95, you can glean the essence of Saliba's instruction by purchasing his newest softcover, Option Spread Strategies: Trading Up, Down and Sideways Markets, with co-authors Karen Johnson and Joe Corona.

Saliba writes with thoroughgoing and comprehensive consideration about options spread strategies, including covered calls, verticals, collars, reverse collars, straddles, strangles, butterflies, condors, calendars, ratio spreads and backspreads.

Option Spread Strategies is a methodical and one could say an academic text because each chapter ends with an exercise, then a quiz. There is even a final exam at the end.

Additionally, a high percentage of the work is devoted to analyzing the Greeks for each spread position.

UNIQUE TECHNIQUES

Saliba's real-world pit background shines through when he discusses some of the techniques that market makers use to go home flat each night, including boxes, conversions, jelly rolls, etc.—concepts that few retail traders employ.

Another plus is that Saliba places emphasis on price forecasting, something that not all "delta-neutral" style strategists do (though they should, because even sideways is a forecast, after all).

He also discusses risk management with assistance from technical analysis concepts, which, again, is not common practice for all DNs. For example, with butterflies and condors, Saliba writes, "As soon as the price action proves the forecast for a directionless market to be incorrect by breaking through a key support or resistance level, one needs to exit the trade"

Note that Saliba does not recommend adjustment to continue with the trade, but rather, just exit. This contrasts with some options pundits who use the deltas on near strikes as exit or roll markers.

But I digress. Indeed, there is an ocean of options advice out there—sometimes for the taking (free webinars) and sometimes for the paying (options mentors, brokers, education firms and academies). But the reader who faithfully works through Option Spread Strategies will know the key concepts and considerations, be able to tackle the markets more expertly and increase his or her knowledge base, thereby enabling the trader to partake in further study or even an advanced training or mentoring program.

John A. Sarkett is the author of best-selling Extraordinary Comebacks: 201 Inspiring Stories of Courage, Triumph, and Success and creator of Option Wizard® software (http://option-wizard.com). He frequently contributes to SFO.

STICKING YOUR NECK OUT

Risk is an inherent component of the investment world, and one that now, more than ever, causes investors anxiety. For these reasons, Curtis M. Faith's book Inside the Mind of the Turtles: How the World's Best Traders Master Risk is both timely and timeless.

Faith writes that the Turtles "looked at risk not as something to be feared and avoided but as something to be respected and understood, because we knew, as did James Bryant Conant, that we could not make progress without sticking our necks out a bit."

In this book, he explains how to develop and profit from a risk-embracing mentality. Faith shares entertaining stories and experiences from his life and career (he earned more than $30 million as a Turtle) that leave little doubt as to the wisdom of his words. Buy it today for $28.95 at SFOmag.com.

By Meghan Pedersen

better **GOOD** than LUCKY

Book Review
August 2010
John A. Sarkett

THE QUANTS UP CLOSE

Card counting is on-the-fly probability analysis. So it makes sense that card counting pioneer Ed Thorp founded what came to be known as quantitative trading, which is probability analysis writ large.

In The Quants: How a New Breed of Math Whizzes Conquered Wall Street and Nearly Destroyed It, Scott Patterson tells Thorp's story, as well as those of the people he influenced:

• Ken Griffin, founder of Citadel

• Cliff Asness of Goldman Sachs and Global Alpha, and AQR Capital Management co-founder

• Boaz Weinstein at Deutsch Bank

• Morgan Stanley's Peter Muller

Patterson peels back layers of secrecy to expose their histories, successes, failures and personal peccadilloes, creating an enjoyable story in the process.

DANGERS

The book does not indict the enterprise of quantitative trading, but it does condemn extreme leverage and its perils.

Patterson follows Thorp, showing how he turns away from overleverage and generates excellent returns without it. For example, System X generated an 18 percent return in 2008 on $36 million. This occurred in a period when Citadel "coughed up half its money, ... AQR fell more than 40 percent, and Saba lost nearly $2 billion."

So we return to the eternal question for Wall Street: Is greed good? Perhaps, like alcohol or fire, a little greed at the right place and time is beneficial if managed. But when overdone, it destroys, leaving everyone on the hook.

The Quants is ambitious, intriguing and provocative—just like the financial industry it covers.

John A. Sarkett is the author of Amazon category bestseller Extraordinary Comebacks: 201 Inspiring Stories of Courage, Triumph, and Success volumes 1 and 2, and the creator of Option Wizard® software.

TRUST YOUR INSTINCTS

—By Meghan Pedersen

In a June 2010 SFO article, Curtis Faith explains the value of pairing right brain attributes with those of the left to achieve optimal results through whole-minded trading. Traders can read even more about the topic in Faith's book Trading from Your Gut.

The text makes clear the value of complementing the more technical strengths of the left brain with the intuition of the right brain. And Faith's careful instructions about using instincts to hone one's trading abilities are filled with scientific explanations, many examples and illustrative charts.

WHAT ARE YOU READING?

Check the new Web column Your Reviews for quick takes from SFO subscribers and post your own. Submit your recommendations.

Book Review
October 2011
John Sarkett

Jeff Augen turns things inside out in his remarkable and challenging book Microsoft Excel for Stock and Option Traders.

He says algorithmic trading has washed away the meaningfulness of familiar tools. "The days of buying and selling stocks when moving averages cross or when an oscillator reaches one side of a channel are over." (Pages 58-59). He proposes using data mining techniques to find "repeating patterns in historical stock market data."

He says to "formulate and test theories until statistically significant results are uncovered" (Page 180). These results must be developed into a trading plan. Augen says many investors have developed successful systems, but he doesn't offer names or examples (Page 52). He does offer tools to find your way.

Augen favors the R-squared tool: "R-squared is obtained by squaring the result of the Pearson product-moment correlation coefficient®" described in a previous chapter. "The Pearson correlation is a measure of linear dependence, while R-squared reveals the percent of the variation in one variable that that is related to variation in the other." (This text is challenging. It will bear repeated readings for those without programming knowledge or degrees in advanced math.)

Augen uses Amazon to illustrate the benefits of buying the stock after a big down day at the tail end of a protracted down move (Page 182).

He doesn't provide his source for historical stock data. (One might be Yahoo. Augen said he uses a subscription to Telechart. It costs $400 to $1,000 per year plus export from TradeStation but typically is free to active traders who use their brokerage.) He doesn't provide a CD, spreadsheets or Visual Basic described in the book. He doesn't cover the waterfront of Excel techniques or Goal Seek or Solver or DDE (Dynamic Data Exchange).

Augen is not the trainer in the gym who fetches and re-racks your dumbbell. He is the gym owner who meets you at 5 a.m. to unlock the door and shows you the equipment. He leaves it to you, assuming you are capable. This will have great appeal and be a revelation to some. Others will be lost. Even the latter should give the book a look to see where they will be headed. It's only a matter of time.

John A. Sarkett created Option Wizard® and Option Wizard® Simplified Options Strategy (SOS) Backtester. He is the author of Extraordinary Comebacks and "Extraordinary Comebacks 2."

Buy Sarkett's book:

Extraordinary Comebacks

Use code **SARK10** to get 10% off and free shipping and handling in continental U.S.

Buy Augen's books:

Microsoft Excel for Stock and Option Traders

Use code **AUGEN1011** to get 20% off and free shipping and handling in the continental U.S.

Email author

Related article

SFO Magazine Department from:
http://www.sfomag.com/Stocks_Futures_Options-Book_Review-dp496i126.aspx

permission is prohibited.

PRODUCT REVIEW

Option Wizard Online 2000

Option Wizard Online 2000 helps traders make better trading decisions by studying volatilities, delta, in-the-money

SARKETT & ASSOCIATES, INC.

Suite 1400
485 Sunset Road
Winnetka, IL 60093
Phone: 847 446-2222
Fax: 941 659-8157
E-mail: info@option-wizard.com
Internet: http://www.option–wizard.com
Product: Options analysis product based on Microsoft Excel spreadsheet.
Equipment requirements: Microsoft Excel 97/98
Price: $399 for delayed and $599 real time; three-month trial for $99. Fully functional one-week trial is free.

by Jayanthi Gopalakrishnan

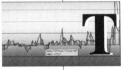

To be able to view a complete and meaningful option analysis in an Excel spreadsheet is intriguing both in terms of the analysis as well as exploring the capabilities of Excel. Option Wizard helps traders make better trading decisions by studying implied and historical volatilities, percent to double, delta, in-the-money probabilities, and several other factors that lend themselves to making better option trading decisions.

Option Wizard has introduced real-time dynamic data exchange (DDE) for eSignal, mytrack.com, PC Quote, and quote.com. Other additions include a "master analysis" button, where you can receive stock price, fundamen-

tal data, options strings, and backtested buy/sell signals with just one click. The product also contains probability graphs and spread tables, as well as Backtest Wizard 4.0, which analyzes 200 days of historical stock prices and provides buy/sell signals and such technical analysis indicators as the force index, moving averages, stochastics, relative strength index (RSI), rate of change (ROC), average directional index (ADX), and directional indicator (DI).

SETUP

Since Option Wizard Online 2000 is an Excel spreadsheet, setting it up is painless. You must download the product from developer Sarkett & Associates' Website. Option Wizard comes in a zip file that you must expand and save on your hard drive; just open up the file the way you would with any other Excel document. Along with the spreadsheet, for an additional $100 fee, you can also get *Options Trading Method*, a 78-page document explaining vari-

ous strategies and methods you may utilize to improve your trading results.

FEATURES

Option Wizard consists of option analytics, decay charts and tables, probability charts, spread tables, strike tables, options-near tables (options close to expiration), options-all tables (all options), position charts/tables, covered-write tables, a spreadsheet to track all your trades, a spreadsheet where you can enter up to 20 stock symbols to monitor (XYZ20), a list of stocks in the Dow Jones Industrial Average (DJIA), Backtest Wizard, volatility tables, and various price and indicator charts. Recently, a new feature was added to the XYZ20 table. Once you enter the 20 symbols into the worksheet, one click on the symbol imports delay or real-time prices and fundamental data. Then you can switch from stock to stock by selecting from a drop-down box. This makes for speedy analysis. Switching from one feature just involves clicking on the specific tab across the bot-

FIGURE 1: OPTION WIZARD ANALYTICS. Once you enter a symbol and hit the refresh or Master Analysis button, the results will be automatically displayed in a spreadsheet, showing a complete analysis of puts and calls.

FIGURE 2: PUT ANALYSIS. The put analysis displays decay tables so you can determine which direction the price of your put option will move as it gets closer to expiration.

tom of the spreadsheet.

The Option Wizard Analytics spreadsheet looks like the display in Figure 1. Here, you see the historical and implied volatilities, decay tables, greeks, delta tables, percent to double, and in-the-money probabilities. The analysis is conducted for both puts and calls. Figure 2 displays the analysis of puts.

You don't need to be an Excel genius to use this product, although some prior knowledge of that software certainly wouldn't hurt. All you have to do is type or paste the stock symbol into the box provided, hit enter, and click on the refresh button. This results in an automatic creation of tables and charts for the current price with all information you would need for a complete option analysis. Examples of the graphs you can find in Option Wizard can be seen in Figures 3 to 5. The force index (Figure 3) is one of the many indicators available in Option Wizard. The probability chart (Figure 4) is a new addition to this version, which displays in-the-money probability of puts and calls as they approach expiration.

To test the capabilities of this program, I analyzed the option activity for February 60 options for Amazon [AMZN]. The price of the underlying was $61.38. After updating the volatility tables, I moved onto the Option Wizard analytics spreadsheet, where I entered the symbol and refreshed the screen. This recalculated everything and produced results specific to the option I had entered. I then clicked on the "calculate implied volatility" button, which calculates the fair value option price for both. The results show a historical volatility for 20, 50, and 100 days to be 110%, 92%, and 89%, respectively. The implied volatility was 63.74% and the fair value option price for the calls was $3.75.

Looking up the quotes for the February 60 calls on the CBOE options-near tables, I found the prices to be between $6-7, which indicated they were overpriced for recent implied volatility but not for 20-50-100-day historical volatilities.

From the click of a few buttons, I can determine several factors that are important to making trading decisions. I can determine how much a $1.00 movement in the price of the underlying would affect the option price, how much the price of the option would change as it got closer to

expiration, and how much the price of the stock would have to move to double the price of the option, the change in delta, and the probability that the option would be in-the-money. All the analyses seemed to indicate that buying February 60 calls was not a good idea.

I skipped over to the Backtest Wizard, where the last signal generated was a short on January 5, 2000, which generated a subsequent six-point profit with no drawdown. (The previous buy signal produced an 18.125-point profit, no drawdown; the most recent signal generated a nine-point loss.) Judging by other indicators such as RSI and stochastics, the stock was oversold, so it wouldn't have been worth it to buy puts or short the stock. It was just a matter of waiting till the signals reversed and generated a buy signal.

SUPPORT

Once I got the program set up, I did not need to contact tech support. After having spoken with other users, I have come to the conclusion that this is a stable and trouble-free product. Those who did have to rely on tech support commented that response time was quick, both by phone and by E-mail. This is a simple program to use, especially if you are familiar with Excel, so you shouldn't need to rely very much on tech support. All you really need to do is enter numbers into certain cells and move from one spreadsheet to another. Not only that, included is a user's manual, so that will help you understand how to use Option Wizard.

CONCLUSION

In general, I was impressed with the features that Option Wizard offers. Many are unique — for just one example, the price-time variant options price table. I do not trade options, but because of the way that this product was set up, I had no difficulty grasping the results it generated. Most users I spoke with said they liked the product for its simplicity and customizability. One of Option Wizard's more popular features is being able to visualize the results of a planned trade on the spreads worksheet just by clicking one of the buttons that represent various scenarios.

Overall? Option Wizard's format and layout, together with all the charts, made it easy to visually determine what factors

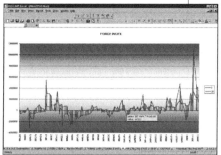

FIGURE 3: FORCE INDEX. The force index is an indicator that focuses on price change, extent of price change, and trading volume. Option Wizard has some charts included, making it easy for users to visualize the performance of indicators.

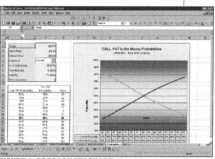

FIGURE 4: PROBABILITY CHART. Here's a graphical representation of in-the-money probabilities of your puts and calls as they approach expiration.

FIGURE 5: POSITION CHART. These display the profit and loss generated as the value of the underlying changes.

to look for when making trading decisions not only for options but also for the underlying security. This is a product that veteran and novice options traders alike will find useful.

Jayanthi Gopalakrishnan is a Staff Writer for STOCKS & COMMODITIES. **S&C**

QUICK-SCANS

SCAN WIZARD
Sarkett & Associates
485 Sunset Road
Winnetka, IL 60093
Phone: 847 446-2222
Fax: 603 754-2565
E-mail: jas@option-wizard.com
Internet: http://option-wizard.com/
scanwizard
Product: Trading system with stock list scanning for trades.
Equipment requirements: Personal computer with Internet access.
Price: $99.95 a month or $995 for a permanent license. Unlimited free trial on restricted lists.

Scan Wizard software scans lists of stock ticker symbols for breakout trend changes, which it then logs in a table with a buy or sell signal based on price, volume, trend, and momentum. It can also create a track record for all buy–sell signals for each and every ticker symbol; chart an issue (candles, force index, and stochastics) (Figure 1); and access news (from Yahoo!) on any ticker symbol.

An Internet product from conception to completion, ScanWizard does not require you, the client, to have a stock datafile on your hard drive; it accesses historical data for any stock directly from Yahoo!. This means you can analyze any stock instantly with no data costs. Scan Wizard comes with lists of the Dow Jones 30, Internet 100, and Standard & Poor's 500; clients may customize and create their own lists as well.

Two sets of buy–sell signals are generated in a huge sortable table:

• **The force index**, developed by Alexander Elder, is a price-volume indicator. When the 20-day force index changes from negative to positive, a buy signal is generated; conversely, when the 20-day force index changes from positive to negative, a sell signal is generated.

• **The triple filter** is more restrictive. It adds conditions (stochastics and moving averages) to the basic force index buy or sell signal and so prevents buying overbought or downtrending stocks (and the reverse for short sales).

You get Scan Wizard by download. Setup is automatic and snafu-free. A free, nonexpiring trial with a fixed ticker list (QQQ, MSFT, INTC, SUNW, ORCL), fixed scan ticker (CSCO), and fixed charting (QQQ) is available as well. The manual is also online.

FIGURE 1: CHARTING. ASH wanders around trying to find direction in late 2000. Scan Wizard's charting package is extremely fast and includes the force index and stochastics, the cornerstones of its scanning criteria.

QUICK-SCANS

While false breakouts in financial markets are numerous, so too are major trend breakouts. Scan Wizard searches for these trend changes as they happen. For example, during the Nasdaq crash of April 2000, Scan Wizard went short the QQQ on both March 29 (110) and April 3 (102.938). The next signal generated was long on May 15 (88.3125) after QQQ hit an interim low of 78 on April 14.

Scan Wizard will generate losing trades as any other indicator or system does. For these, traders must apply money management discipline. All gains and losses are logged into the program to provide you with a track record of

previous signals for the past 200 days. That said, interpreting the output isn't duck-simple: the programming sometimes overwrites the screens you want

---

ScanWizard accesses historical data for any stock directly from Yahoo!. This means you can analyze any stock instantly with no data costs.

---

to see, but the windows are named by the ticker symbol, so you can locate the ticker and window you are looking for. There is a summary of backtest results on each ticker screen, but no overall win-loss compilation, or ability to rank.

We were told this ability would be forthcoming in Scan Wizard shortly.

In addition, the meaning of "10-day max gain" and "10-day max loss" is ambiguous, but the explanation of such is available on the online manual, and it clears up the confusion.

The software performs perfectly in close collaboration with Internet sources, principally Yahoo!. Everything is disclosed and it's going to find any significant changes in trend — along with lots of back-and-forth. Absent a long-term track record but with an unending free trial, traders should check Scan Wizard out by following it.

—*John Sweeney, Interim Editor*

S&C

■ TRADER'S NOTEBOOK

WORKING-MONEY.COM

Trading And "Moneyball"

What do baseball and trading have in common? More than you would have thought.

by John A. Sarkett

Can an individual retail trader venture into the marketplace, take on elite, highly paid hedge fund managers, mutual fund managers, market makers, and other assorted professionals, and come out ahead? A new book that is all the buzz in Chicago trading circles would say "yes."

Moneyball: The Art Of Winning An Unfair Game, by Michael Lewis (his other books include *Liar's Poker)*, tells the unlikely story of one Billy Beane, a supertalented professional baseball player who never achieved his potential in the major leagues, who changed course and then, in a most unlikely turnabout, became the most successful general manager in baseball. He did it by forming a fundamentally different and iconoclastic view of the game, one that is built on a statistical foundation of *what actually works.*

You must read this book to absorb the full weight of the evidence, but to whet your appetite, here are the salient points that you can apply directly to your financial market operations.

ANDREW VANDERKARR

WHAT'S THE STORY?

Once upon a time, Billy Beane was the top prospect in major league baseball. Regarded as more gifted than 95% of professional players playing at the time, he signed at 16. In baseball parlance, he had the "hose" (arm), "wheels" (speed), body to do it all, and the "Good Face" — that is, the look of a baseball god. He was, as one scout remarked, "a player you could dream on."

In accordance with the adage, "Life is what happens when you are making other plans," it was all downhill from there. Much later, Beane came to realize he didn't really enjoy playing baseball, was never comfortable with the pressure, and had signed on and played for the money only.

After bouncing around the majors and the minors, he quit at 27 to become a scout — a move that was unheard of. Unlike most baseball front office types, Beane's mentor, Oakland A's general manager Sandy Alderson, was not a baseball player in his past life, but had been instead an attorney and Marine officer, who believed in systems and science. And soon enough, so did Beane.

Beane would become a general manager himself at 35. He

was aided indirectly by several notable statisticians, individuals like Bill James, who published the *Baseball Abstract* series, annual volumes of hitherto-overlooked statistics, facts, and analysis on baseball, and directly by Paul DePodesta, who was then Beane's assistant in the A's organization. There were even some consulting companies retained along the way, one specializing in arcane baseball analysis, the Society for American Baseball Research (SABR).

This was all most unorthodox. To most powers that be in baseball, the sport was art, indefinable. To Billy Beane and his various bean counters, it was science. Collectively, they became the equivalent of card counters, the "Einsteins of baseball," armed with new evidence and able to see the national pastime in new and startling ways. Here are just a few tenets of their "new" way of analyzing the sport:

1 The single most important thing in the game is to not make an out.

2 As such, bunts, and "hit and run" plays were highly overrated, as were "manufacturing runs."

3 Patience mattered: patience to walk, for example. On-base percentage is more important than batting average.

4 "Taking" the first pitch puts the odds of a successful at-bat in the hands of the batter.

5 Batters can create walks by deciding which pitches to swing at.

6 Pitchers who know how to strike out batters can often be more valuable than 100 mile-per-hour hurlers. The market, however, values the latter more highly. Beane traded these individuals whenever it was to his advantage.

All of the above were *proven* statistically, and only statistically. The naked eye could not discern these facts, Beane and his counters realized. Did it work?

Beane's amazing win-loss record as general manager of the Oakland A's went like this:

- 1998: 74 wins, 88 losses
- 1999: 87 wins, 76 losses
- 2000: 91 wins, 70 losses
- 2001: 102 wins, 60 losses
- 2002: 103 wins, 59 losses
- 2003: 99 wins, 66 losses

Did the A's have the stars? No, just the opposite. The Yankees paid their players between $50 million and $100 million *more* than the A's *each year.*

It wasn't the money, it was management. The *system* was the star.

Great. What's this got to do with trading?

THE SYSTEM IS THE STAR

Many traders flit from idea to idea, tip to tip, hot market to hot market. When it doesn't work, they take the blame personally. So instead, ask yourself: What is your system? What is your edge? Who are you earning your dollars in the market from and why? If you can't state your system in one sentence or two, you don't have one. Beane's offensive system: get on base, score runs. Defense: get batters out. Sounds simple, doesn't it? But most baseball managers are more fixated on effect versus cause: 100 mile-per-hour "heat," being aggressive at the plate, speed on the base paths. Beane looked past these ancient yardsticks to actual results.

So what works? Does your system work? Can you prove it? *Probabilities: put them to work for you.* In your trading, stack the odds in your favor: fundamentals, technicals, then options analysis.

Here's an example. You want to be long a stock. Instead of choosing an overvalued candidate, one that's already run up and garnered its share of attention in the media, look for an overlooked candidate. Here's an example. At this writing, Liberty Media (L) sells for just under $9 a share. Analysts put the break-up value of the company (which holds stakes in News Corp., Time Warner, shopping network QVC, and others) some 20% to 30% higher. So the fundamentals are there. It has traded recently in a band of $10 to $12. Next, use technical analysis (stochastics, relative strength index [RSI], and so forth) to spot oversold buy points. Finally, use options to generate leverage and/or risk management.

With those simple actions, you just put the odds in your favor three ways: fundamentals, technicals, and options. Doing so doesn't guarantee you the win, but it's a world of difference from taking uncalculated risks.

TRADING THE BILLY BEANE WAY

Still not convinced? Take another look, comparing baseball played the Billy Beane way and trading:

Backtest. Go back in time. How would the strategy you are proposing have worked across time? To trade your system, you must have confidence. What was the win/loss percentage, drawdowns, and all the rest? Make this process part of your routine.

See the same things everybody else does but in a different way. Most managers pine after big, strong 100 mph hurlers. But when Billy Beane would get one, as often as not, he would trade the pitcher. He looked for real-results players, sometimes chubby, out-of-shape players whom other teams spurned. What does this tell you? Be a hedge fund yourself; "sell" the overpriced securities, buy the obscure and overlooked. Too many traders only look for the long side of a market. Rewards on the short side can be faster and more dramatic. *Think two ways.*

> What is your system? What is your edge? If you can't state your system in one sentence or two, you don't have one.

Maintain a positive psychology. When Beane was a player, he was a mental mess. Bullpen pitchers would come down to the dugout for one of his at-bats just to see what destruction he would wreak when he struck out. As a foil, in *Moneyball*, Lewis profiled Beane's teammate Len Dykstra as "...able to instantly forget any failure and draw strength from every success. He had no concept of failure." One time, Beane and Dykstra were watching Baseball Hall of Famer Steve Carlton warm up. Dykstra didn't recognize the pitching legend and asked who he was. When Beane told him, Dykstra replied that he could get a hit off him. "I'll stick him," he said. Then he went out and did it.

Beane did have one good mental trait: he never allowed himself to become sentimental about a game, a player, or his own experiences. Translating that trait to the markets would be: "Ours is not to reason why, ours is just to sell and buy." Enter your stops or buy your puts, and if it goes, it goes.

Don't do it (just) for the money. After Beane became the most successful general manager in baseball, he worked a notable trade: himself, to the Boston Red Sox organization, for $12.5 million over five years. The deed done, he couldn't go through with it. After his misshapen baseball career as a player, he had vowed to never do anything just for the money again. He was loyal to the A's, to his job, to his life in Oakland. He still had the dream of winning the World Series, and all that would mean to the validation of his ideas. So he stuck with the A's.

Similarly, there are other rewards for trading, some psychic: As Bill James wrote in his *1988 Baseball Abstract*: "It is a wonderful thing to know you are right and the world is wrong."

With probabilities, system, and method working for you, you can have a chance to know this feeling, directly, for yourself in your trading.

John A. Sarkett is the developer of Option Wizard Scan and Scan Wizard software (http://option-wizard.com).

SUGGESTED READING

James, Bill [2003]. *The 2004 Bill James Handbook*, ACTA Publications.
_____ [1988]. *1988 Baseball Abstract*, Ballantine Books.
Lewis, Michael [2004]. *Moneyball: The Art Of Winning An Unfair Game*, WW Norton & Co.
_____ [1990]. *Liar's Poker: Rising Through The Wreckage On Wall Street*, Penguin Books.
Surowiecki, James [2002]. "The Buffett Of Baseball," *The New Yorker*: September 23.
http://option-wizard.com

†*See Traders' Glossary for definition*

S&C

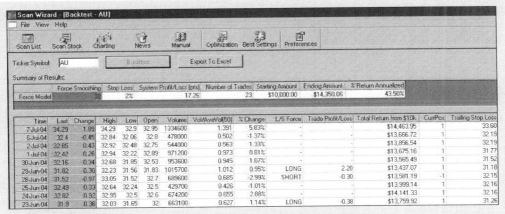

TRADING SYSTEMS

A mechanical, statistically based trading system — like Scan Wizard (shown), which was devised by the author — can help take the emotion out of trading and allow you to focus on what actually works over time. Consider purchasing or creating an optimizable system that provides buy/sell signals (both long and short), exit points, and trailing stops. The program should also keep a track record.

Using Sample Variance

Backtesting Option Strategies

Looking for a quick way to backtest option strategies? You can use Excel to count occurrences of historical prices outside a price band you set to develop an expectation for future price movement. Here's how.

by John A. Sarkett

 So much of the option trader's life has been enhanced over just the past 10 or so years. We have radically lower commissions — $0.15 to $1.50 per contract, plus various ticket charge plans; we have tighter markets, with high-volume contracts just one penny apart; we have better software with risk curves, what-if scenarios, and charting, with brokers and vendors continuing to enhance their offerings; and finally, we have easier access to futures and world markets for intermarket hedging.

Only one aspect of the option trading experience remains, more or less, as it was years ago — option strategy backtesting. If I put on this SPX or SPY or RUT or ETF or XYZ butterfly, condor, calendar, or double diagonal, what are my chances of success based on the recent past? That is the biggest question for every option trader.

For a back-of-the-envelope type calculation, some use deltas as shorthand for the probability of going in-the-money. For example, an option with a 10 delta will have roughly a 10% chance of doing so. Actual probability math is much more complex (see my December 1997 S&C article), but the answers usually come out close enough. Some software calculates "probability of expiration" or "probability of touching" (strike) for you. Thinkorswim does this, for example.

Other traders take on a much more time-consuming task of establishing the trade in their option software, then clicking through, day by day, to see how the trade progresses. This allows you to insert "adjustments" and see how these fare. Many option traders have invested many weekend hours in this kind of research.

Industrial strength option packages provide this opportunity; OptionVue is still the gold standard, although there are new offerings, too. Typical time involved for just one ticker: one year's worth of data can be analyzed in 30 to 60 minutes. The data accessed is typically real, historical option data. (In the case of missing data, some software programs will insert theoretical prices.)

KEY EXCEL FORMULAS FOR VARIANCE

You can build your own variance spreadsheet or find one to try at http://option-wizard.com. Here are the key formulas:

• Access five years of historical data from web sources (say, Yahoo) in a spreadsheet.

• Use the offset function of Excel to determine change from today to "x" days back.

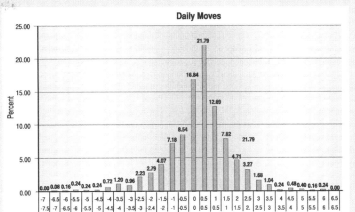

Daily Moves

e.g. =(H1265/OFFSET(H1265,-BO2,0))-1

Use the IF function in Excel to determine if the particular day's change is outside the band you set:

=IF(BP1265<BR2,BP1265,)

Use conditional formatting to highlight moves outside the bands.

Use COUNTIF to count how many times the day's close exceeds the bands:

=COUNTIF(BQ10:BQ1500,">0")

Divide it by the number of days surveyed.

SIMPLE SAMPLE VARIANCE

Is there a faster or cheaper way? There is: simple sample variance and the power of good old Microsoft Excel. Simply put, sample variance will tell you how many times XYZ exceeded 5% up or 4% down in 35 days — or whatever your parameters are — over an extended time period — for example, five years.

There is a tradeoff. In an analysis like this that takes just a few seconds, there is no provision for adjustments and how the trade would fare. (An option adjustment is the adding of an additional position or position(s) to the original position in order to protect or enhance profitability.) In addition, instead of using real option data, the strategist would use actual historical prices of the underlying.

Having listed these caveats, my research tells me many option traders would trade 30 to 60 minutes of logging prospective adjustments, and the use of real option data for a five-second look at how a particular strategy might perform on a particular underlying.

That said, here's how to use sample variance to analyze the prospect of probability for your option trade. The strategist would establish a time frame of a theoretical trade, for example, 25 days, and price bands that would contain profit, for example, up or down 5%. He or she could pose the question of how often the underlying moves outside this band in the chosen time period, say, over the last five years, and then let Excel tally the occurrences. Divide these by the total

number of days, and you have the answer — one that would give a quick indication of the odds of success of any option strategy's probability of staying above breakeven, based on what actually happened over the last five years (see sidebar, "Key Excel Formulas For Variance"). So instead of spending an hour, you would have an answer about as quickly as you can point and click.

Date	SPY CLOSE	PRICE "X" DAYS AGO, IN THIS CASE, 46 DAYS AGO	VARIANCE: CLOSE/CLOSE MINUS 46
Tue-25-Aug-09	103.16	92.22	0.1186
Wed-26-Aug-09	103.17	92.04	0.1209
Thu-27-Aug-09	103.40	89.28	0.1582
Fri-28-Aug-09	103.38	89.35	0.1570
Mon-31-Aug-09	102.46	90.12	0.1369
Tue-1-Sep-09	100.20	92.08	0.0882
Wed-2-Sep-09	99.82	91.84	0.0869
Thu-3-Sep-09	100.65	92.70	0.0858
Fri-4-Sep-09	102.06	91.95	0.1100
Tue-8-Sep-09	102.94	92.33	0.1149
Wed-9-Sep-09	103.73	89.81	0.1550
Thu-10-Sep-09	104.79	89.80	0.1669
Fri-11-Sep-09	104.77	88.06	0.1898
Mon-14-Sep-09	105.28	88.00	0.1964
Tue-15-Sep-09	105.72	88.17	0.1990
Wed-16-Sep-09	107.32	87.96	0.2201
Thu-17-Sep-09	107.16	90.10	0.1893
Fri-18-Sep-09	106.72	90.61	0.1778
Mon-21-Sep-09	106.45	93.26	0.1414
Tue-22-Sep-09	107.07	93.11	0.1499
Wed-23-Sep-09	106.18	94.13	0.1280
Thu-24-Sep-09	105.01	95.13	0.1039
Fri-25-Sep-09	104.45	95.57	0.0929
Mon-28-Sep-09	106.32	95.55	0.1127
Tue-29-Sep-09	106.00	97.66	0.0854
Wed-30-Sep-09	105.59	98.06	0.0768
Thu-1-Oct-09	102.97	98.35	0.0470
Fri-2-Oct-09	102.49	97.89	0.0470
Mon-5-Oct-09	104.02	97.65	0.0652
Tue-6-Oct-09	105.51	98.67	0.0693
Wed-7-Oct-09	105.80	98.81	0.0707
Thu-8-Oct-09	106.61	100.44	0.0614
Fri-9-Oct-09	107.26	100.70	0.0651
Mon-12-Oct-09	107.68	100.41	0.0724
Tue-13-Oct-09	107.46	99.89	0.0758
Wed-14-Oct-09	109.31	101.20	0.0801
Thu-15-Oct-09	109.71	100.99	0.0863
Fri-16-Oct-09	108.89	99.73	0.0918
Mon-19-Oct-09	109.79	100.80	0.0892
Tue-20-Oct-09	109.21	101.57	0.0752
Wed-21-Oct-09	108.23	100.79	0.0738
Thu-22-Oct-09	109.33	98.31	0.1121
Fri-23-Oct-09	108.08	99.09	0.0907

OPTION WIZARD

FIGURE 1: BREAKING OUT. Once a bull market run began here in the SPY, it exceeded the daily variance bands (that is, last price was constantly equal to or greater than 7.5% versus price 46 days earlier) nearly every day for two months; there was no regression for those waiting for a pullback — an important consideration for the option trader who must be alert and nimble, and typically does not have one or two years, like a long-term position trader, for a position to come back.

APPLYING IT

Does sample variance matter in the real world of trading? It does. As an example, quite a few option traders trade the Russell 2000 as a condor vehicle each month, only vaguely realizing it is often more volatile as the Standard & Poor's 500. (If you do trade it anyway, do the premiums compensate? Short answer: Depends on where the market is. It pays to do a bit of due diligence.)

In this particular example, SPY or SPX vs. the volatile RUT, a quick study of variance would tell the option trader which is more volatile. It should not come as a surprise, then, that for many who trade the RUT month after month with delta-neutral strategies that profit when the RUT stands still out of nothing more than habit, the results have been less than sterling in the recent past.

That's the competitive edge — working *against* them, since they are not fully aware. As of this writing, May 2011, over the past five years, the SPY close exceeded the close 46 days ago by 7.5% exactly 20.05% of the time; for RUT, 24.88%. Going the other way, in SPY, the close has been 7.5% or more lower than that of 46 days ago, exactly 17.60% of the time; in RUT, 16.12%. Sometimes, small caps (RUT, Russell 2000) are in the ascendant, while sometimes they lag; the key is to be aware of the recent environment, and place your option strategy accordingly.

Here's another example. You have in mind to earn some income with a calendar spread on Big Pharma. Until recently, Merck (MRK) retained much of its luster, while Pfizer (PFE) was looked down on. Which stock is more stable? Using the same measure, incidence of greater than or less than 5% moves up or down in 50+ days, we find:

- MRK: 63.57%

- PFE: A higher 69%

- How about a stock that gets less media attention — Eli Lilly & Co. (LLY): Bingo! 43.78%

Armed with three measurements on three candidates, the strategist can give a look to particular option strategy prices for particular companies and compare with a more fully formed perspective. Or if you do choose MRK or PFE, having specific insight into the sample variance for each will prepare the trader for quicker and more meaningful adjustments on the wider mover — for example, turning a calendar into a double calendar.

This type of strategy testing shows one other important thing, especially for those who like to dig in their heels. And you can see it on a spreadsheet (Figure 1).

Prices that move outside of 5% or 7% or 10% bands "x" days ago are often breaking out, either to the upside or downside. It pays to exit at breakeven, or adjust and play again another day, and protect your option principal. Bodies in motion tend

"At bat is number 8, Sidonski, who leads the league in home runs, RBIs, and product endorsement fees."

> **Everyone has to do their own due diligence, everyone has to come to their own conclusions. Tools like sample variance will help you do that.**

to stay in motion, right through and beyond expiration. Bodies at rest tend to stay at rest.

TIME

Go out one more expiration and there is only a 42% chance that MRK will stay within the 5% borders set here by the option strategist. There is a 58% chance that it will move beyond the bands set. That might suggest another strategy — if volatilities were sufficiently low, buying a straddle, a strangle, or a debit spread, and expecting MRK to follow its historical precedent and, in fact, *move out of its 5% bounds.*

Everyone has to do their own due diligence; everyone has to come to their own conclusions. Tools like sample variance will help you do that, quickly, easily, and inexpensively.

A quick study of variance provides either confirmation of additional fundamental and technical research, or the jumping-off point for same. Perhaps the most important part of the whole enterprise here is not any single calculation or any one trade, but putting five years' worth of probabilities in your favor. If you know that a given option strategy should be successful nine out of 12 months, and you decide to try it but lose the first month, get discouraged, and don't return for months 2 and 3 and 4, where you would have likely been profitable, your probability of failure becomes 100%. And no one wants to undertake *that* probability.

John A. Sarkett designed Option Wizard software (http://option-wizard.com). He writes frequently for the financial press, and has written for STOCKS & COMMODITIES since 1995. His nonfiction work Extraordinary Comebacks *is an Amazon bestseller. Go to Sarkett.com for a full set of his titles, including Option Wizard Trading Method.*

SUGGESTED READING

Sarkett, John [1997]. "Time And Options Probabilities," *Technical Analysis of* STOCKS & COMMODITIES, Volume 15: December.

‡OptionWizard

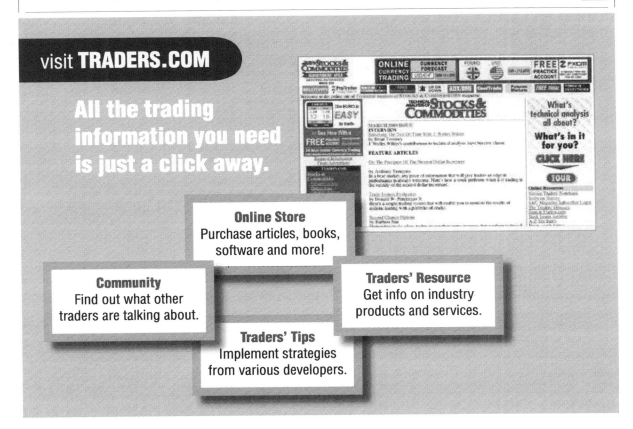

The Force Index

By John A. Sarkett, Developer, <u>Option Wizard</u>

Prices undulate like ocean waves.

Ebb and flow, flow and ebb.

Every once in a while, however, a huge shift in price and volume hits the market with the impact of a tidal wave. This sets the stage for follow-through price movement. There is an indicator that measures and depicts this Major Event more vividly than any other: the Force Index. Developed by Dr. Alexander Elder, it is presented in his latest book *Trading for a Living.*

The Force Index focuses on three key pieces of market information -- price change, extent of price change and trading volume. The force of every move is defined by its direction, distance, and volume. If prices close higher, the force is positive, if lower, then negative. The greater the change in prices, the greater the force. The greater the volume, the greater the force. That is the simple but powerful concept behind Force Index.

Like other oscillators, Force Index works best if it is smoothed with a moving average (MA). Force Index smoothed with a short MA , e.g. two days, helps pinpoint entry and exit points. Force Index smoothed with a longer MA, e.g. 13 days, shows major change in the force of bulls and bears.

Building the Force Index

You can build your own Force Index database for any security or index in a spreadsheet. Here is the formula:

Force Index = Volume Today * (Close Today - Close Yesterday)

Let's look at a spreadsheet to get the 'feel' for the numbers; here are the numbers for the Nikkei Dow:

<u>Nikkei Dow</u>

Date Close Volume Force Index FI: 2-ema FI: 13-ema

THE NIKKEI DOW					
Date	Close	Volume	Force index	FI: 2-EMA	FI: 13-EMA
10/29	25329	3834			
10/30	25242	4495	-391065		
10/31	25194	1372	-65856	-130807	
11/01	24295	2547	-2289753	-1570105	
110/2	24195	2891	-289100	-7161902	
11/05	24385	1448	275120	-55287	
11/06	23966	2796	-1171524	-799445	
11/07	23500	3675	-1712550	-1408182	
11/08	22970	3167	-1678510	-1588400	
11/09	22932	2880	-109440	-602426	
11/13	23974	2484	2588328	1524743	
11/14	23937	1827	-67599	463181	
11/15	23487	2212	-995400	-509206	
11/16	23172	2741	-863415	-745345	-338231
11/19	23519	1931	670057	198256	-261590
11/20	23205	1405	-441170	-228027	-256796
11/21	22816	2259	-878751	-661843	-314660
11/22	23400	2163	1263192	621514	-180921

(If you like to plot the numbers yourself, or import them from a technical analysis program for your own analysis, here's a programmer's trick to make the Force Index exponential moving average (EMA) numbers smaller and more chartable: divide Force Index by the price of the underlying security.)

If you plot Force Index as a histogram, you will see it is quite jagged, so Dr. Elder recommends smoothing it with a 2-day-average and a 13-day-average. Short term traders can buy when the 2-day exponential moving average (ema) is negative and sell when it is positive, as long as you trade with the 13-day ema of prices, that is to say, trade with the trend, buying uptrends and selling downtrends.

The 13-day EMA of Force Index tracks longer-term change in the force of bulls and bears. When it crosses above its centerline, it shows that the bulls have the upper hand. Conversely, when it turns negative and heads down through the centerline, it shows that the bears are in control.

Divergences between a 13-day EMA of Force Index and prices point to important turning points. It shows that bulls or bears are losing their firing power (volume) and that a counterattack may soon follow.

Seven Trading Rules

A 2-day EMA of Force Index is a highly sensitive indicator of the short-term force of bulls and bears. It is so sensitive that it is best used to fine-tune signals of other indicators. When a trend-following indicator identifies an uptrend, the declines of the 2-day EMA of Force Index spot the best buying points. When a trend-following tool identifies a downtrend, a 2-day EMA of Force Index pinpoints the best shorting areas.

Rule NO. 1.

Buy when a 2-day EMA of Force Index turns negative during uptrends.

No matter how fast and furious an uptrend, there are always pullbacks. If you delay buying until the 2-day EMA of Force Index turns negative, you will buy closer to a short-term bottom.

Buy-Stop, Sell-Stop Trading Tactic. When a 2-day EMA of Force Index turns negative during an uptrend, place a buy order above the high price of that day. If the uptrend resumes and prices rally, you will be stopped in on the long side. If prices continue to decline, your order will not be executed. Then lower your buy order to within one tick of the high of the latest bar. Once your buy stop is triggered, placed a protective stop below the low of the trade day or the previous day, whichever is lower. This tight stop is seldom touched in a strong uptrend, but gets you out early if the trend is weak.

Now for our second rule . . .

Rule NO. 2

Sell short when a 2-day EMA of Force Index turns positive in downtrends.

Your trend-following indicators identify a downtrend, but rather than short the lows, wait until your 2-day EMA of Force Index turns positive. It indicates a quick splash of bullishness -- a shorting opportunity. Place your order to sell short below the low of the latest price bar.

Let's say, however, the 2-day EMA of Force Index continues to rally after you place your sell order, raise it daily to within a tick of the latest bar's low. Once price slide and you go short, place a protective stop above the high of the latest price bar or the previous bar, whichever is higher. Move your stop down to a break-even level as early as possible, (remembering of course, that while various trading systems can be successful at various times, money management is the one system we all must have all the time to be successful.)

The 2-day EMA of Force Index helps you determine when to pyramid your positions. You can add to longs in uptrends each time Force Index turns negative and add to shorts in downtrends whenever Force Index turns positive.

Force Index even provides a glimpse into the future. When a 2-day EMA of Force Index falls to its lowest low in a month, it shows that bears are strong and prices are likely to fall even lower. When a 2-day EMA of Force Index rallies to its highest level in a month, it shows that bulls are strong and prices are likely to rise even higher.

Perhaps most helpfully for some, a 2-day EMA of Force Index helps you decide when to close a position. A short term trader who goes short when this indicator is positive should cover when it turns negative. A longer-term trader should exit only if a trend changes (as demonstrated by a change in the slope of a 13-day EMA of price), or if there is a divergence between 2-day EMA of Force Index and the trend.

Rule NO. 3

Buy when prices fall to a new low while Force Index makes a more shallow bottom.

Bullish divergences between 2-day EMA of Force Index and price give strong buy signals. A bullish divergence occurs when prices fall to a new low while Force Index makes a more shallow bottom.

Rule NO. 4

Sell when prices rally to a new high while Force Index traces a lower second top.

Bearish divergences between 2-day EMA of Force Index and price give strong sell signals. A bearish divergence occurs when prices rally to anew high while Force Index makes a lower second top.

Looking at the intermediate term

A 13-day EMA of Force Index identifies longer-term changes in the strength of bulls and bears. Its position relative to its centerline show which group is in control. When it diverts from price movement, major turning points are identified.

Rule NO. 5

When a 13-day EMA of Force Index is above the centerline, bulls control the market, and when it is below the centerline, bears control it. When this indicator flutters near its centerline, it identifies a trendless market -- a warning not to use trend-following trading methods.

When a rally commences, prices often leap up on heavy volume. When a 13-day EMA of Force Index reaches a new high, it confirms the uptrend. When the uptrend ages, prices rise more slowly or volume becomes thinner. Then a 13-day EMA of Force Index starts tracing lower tops and eventually drops below its centerline. It signals that the bull move is over.

Rule NO. 6

A new peak in the 13-day EMA of Force Index shows that a rally is likely to continue. A bearish divergence between a 13-day EMA of Force Index and prices give gives a strong signal to sell short. If prices reach a new high but this indicator traces a lower peak, it warns that bulls are losing power and bears are ready to take control.

Rule NO. 7

A new low in the 13-day EMA of Force Index shows that a downtrend is likely to continue. If prices fall to a new low but this indicator traces a more shallow low, it warns that bears are losing power. This bullish divergence gives a strong buy signal.

When a downtrend begins, prices usually drop on heavy volume. When a 13-day EMA of Force Index falls to new lows, it confirms the decline. As the downtrend grows old, prices fall more slowly or volume dries up. Then the 13-day EMA of Force Index starts making more shallow bottoms and finally rallies above its centerline. It shows that the back of the bear has been broken.

One final caveat: the Force Index is not perfect, nor is any other indicator. It is best used to confirm other indicators, and when it is wrong, or when it is misinterpreted, your money management skills should preserve your capital for future opportunities.

Authors

This feature is based on material from "Trading for a Living" by Dr. Alexander Elder. Dr. Elder has published more than 50 articles, software, and book reviews, and spoke at numerous financial conferences. In 1988, he founded Financial Trading Seminars, Inc., an educational firm for traders (800.458.0939 or fax 718.639.8889). Dr. Elder offers his expert commentary on CNBC from time to time.

John A. Sarkett is the developer of Option Wizard and writes on and is active in the financial markets.

Visuals, examples

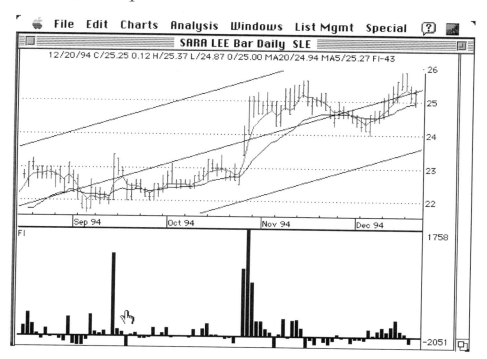

Sara Lee (SLE)

Rule NO. 1.

Buy when a 2-day EMA of Force Index turns negative during uptrends.

With the moving averages pointed up, on Sept. 20, 1994, SLE declined enough to turn Force Index negative (-2051, to be exact). Applying Dr. Elder's rule of putting your buy stop above that day's high, you would have bought SLE at 22.75 on Sept. 30, 1994. Subsequent market action would have created a loss of just 3/8ths of a point, but then followed with an advance to 25.125 on November 15, 1994 -- a 10% gain in six weeks.

Gap (GPS)

Rule NO. 2

Sell short when a 2-day EMA of Force Index turns positive in downtrends. (See cursor.)

Rule NO. 3

Buy when prices fall to a new low while Force Index makes a more shallow bottom. (See Gap September low and high lows for FI).

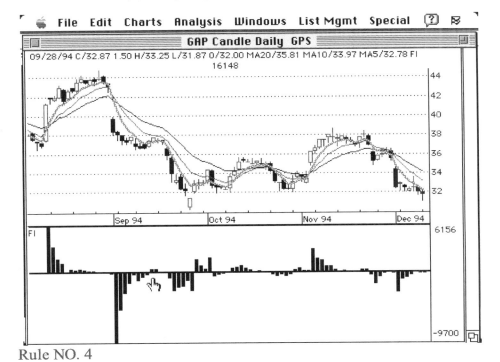

Rule NO. 4

Sell when prices rally to a new high while Force Index traces a lower second top. (See November highs at 38 and decline in FI.)

Rule NO. 7

A new low in the 13-day EMA of Force Index shows that a downtrend is likely to continue. If prices fall to a new low but this indicator traces a more shallow low, it warns that bears are losing power. This bullish divergence gives a strong buy signal. For example, early in September, the Gap plunged to 38, made new lows in the Force Index, which forecast still lower lows ahead, down to the 31 level.

With the Gap, Inc. headed south, on September 14, 1994, Force Index turned positive (3124). A short at 37.50 would ensue, and there was to be no drawdown on the position whatsoever, all the way down to a low of 30.125 on September 27, 1994, just 13 days later. A similar signal crops up at this point. A conservative trader might have passed on it, reasoning that a one-month decline of 44 to 30 represented most of the shorting opportunity, but let's say our hypothetical trader took the trade anyway, at let's say, 32.25. With a stop-loss at 34 in the cross-over area, the net for the two trades would be approximately seven points plus, two points minus for a gain of 5 points or some 15% in approximately one month.

As for rule 3, buy on new lows but shallower Force Index, the end-of-September prices in the 31s, offers a run to 38 in six weeks.

Force Index rules also counsel to get out at this level, rule 4, because the new highs of 38 are not confirmed by new highs in the Force Index, in fact, Force Index steadily declines, presaging the decline back to the 31s in December.

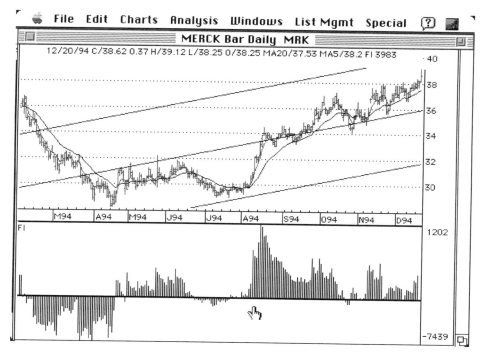

Merck (MRK) and the 13-day e.m.a. of Force Index

Rule NO. 5

When a 13-day EMA of Force Index is above the centerline, bulls are in control of the market, and when it is below the centerline, bears are in control.

Rule NO. 6

A new peak in the 13-day EMA of Force Index shows that a rally is likely to continue (see cursor). A bearish divergence between a 13-day EMA of Force Index and prices give gives a strong signal to sell short. If prices reach a new high but this indicator traces a lower peak, it warns that bulls are losing power and bears are ready to take control.

After many months of concern over Pres. Clinton's health care plan and the negative effect it would have on drug companies, the bears began losing power to push prices down further in April, 1994. When neither Force Index nor prices could make new lows in July, the stage was set for a run from the 29s to 38 in the next six months.

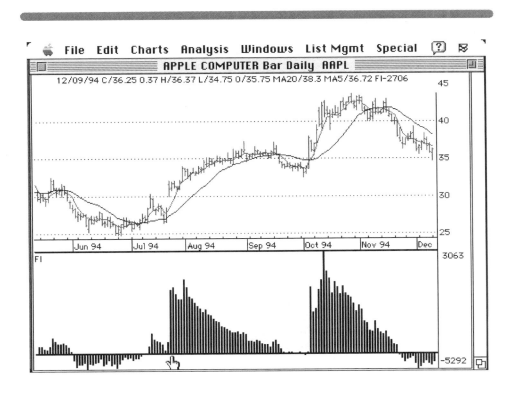

Force Index: a visual difference

Why Force Index?

The reason is visual. While oscillators like stochastics, relative strength index and commodity channel index are extremely valuable, and few of us would want to trade without them, there is a certain sameness, a certain gradualness about their undulating waves. As these are price-only based indicators, there is no difference in them if 50,000 or 5,000,000 shares or contracts are traded.

With Force Index, there is a difference, and often a powerful difference.

Take a look at how the 13-day e.m.a of Force Index confirmed last year's upmove in Apple Computer.

The Force Index is not a long-term indicator, as evidenced as the subsequent slippage in Apple stock, it is a trading tool, but it did confirm the change in direction for the following 13 points, and 90 days from the first July signal.

Like the four players in the ancient Oriental play Roshomon, who tell very different versions of the same incident, different traders can look at a single chart and come to very different conclusions about the direction of the market. Therefore, what typically follows is the ebb and flow of the market, up and down, bull push and bear pull.

What the Force Index does is show clearly, dramatically and compellingly, when the bulls or the bears have broken through decisively, and a market consensus is reached that will provide the path of least resistance for trading days immediately following. It is dramatic, visual and compelling, and that's why I decided to include it in the most recent Personal Analyst and Personal Hotline!

Charts courtesy Trendsetter Software Inc., Personal Analyst 2.0 Reprinted with permission from Technical Analysis of STOCKS & COMMODITIES™ magazine.
© 1995 Technical Analysis, Inc., (800) 832-4642, http://www.traders.com

MARKET MENTORS

New!
From the author of Option Wizards®:
real life success stories from the
financial markets, comprehensive
treatment of 20+ programs, 300 pages

$23.95 PUBLISHER DIRECT
includes shipping

Go the next step: Comprehensively
survey the burgeoning field of
market mentors, their methods,
strategies, and what their students
say.

This is a must read before you plunk
down your hard-won cash to join any program. Sorts out this new
cottage industry taken up by brokers, small companies and one-man
shops.

Emphasis on options education, which started some 20 years ago,
gained widespread interest some 10 years ago, and grown steadily
since then.

This new book surveyed the field initially several years ago, and then
again in 2012, to catalog changes. The consummation of hundreds of
hours of research, MARKET MENTORS covers some 21 programs
whose fees range from free to $25,000, from major brokers and
institutions, to one man shops, and all points in between.

Conclusions? As with other professions, there is a vast range of
approach from mentor to mentor. While a newcomer to markets and
options can benefit from mentoring, the author recommends: study the
field, then ask questions. And then be prepared for hard work, lots of it.
Trading is not an easy way to earn money, those who tell you it is
should have one mark against them from the outset. This book will put
you way ahead of the curve, and save costly errors.

Buy publisher direct ($23.95, includes shipping) vs. Amazon price
($25) at http://option-wizard.com.

Made in the USA
Lexington, KY
30 April 2013